THE NOTEBOOKS OF RAYMOND CHANDLER

and

English Summer

A Gothic Romance

by

Raymond Chandler

Illustrated by Edward Gorey

Edited by Frank MacShane

THE ECCO PRESS
NEW YORK

First published by The Ecco Press in 1976
26 West 17th Street, New York, NY 10011

Published simultaneously in Canada by
Penguin Books Canada Ltd., Ontario

Library of Congress Cataloging in Publication Data
Chandler, Raymond, 1888–1959.
  [Notebooks of Raymond Chandler]
  The notebooks of Raymond Chandler: and, English summer: a gothic romance
/ by Raymond Chandler; illustrated by Edward Gorey; edited by
Frank MacShane.
     p.   cm.
  1. Chandler, Raymond, 1888–1959—Notebooks, sketchbooks, etc.
  I. MacShane, Frank.   II. Chandler, Raymond, 1888–1959. English summer.
1991. III. Title.
PS3505.H3224A6   1991   813´.52—dc20   90-23510CIP
ISBN 0-88001-270-6: $9.95

Printed in the United States of America

Acknowledgments:

  Antaeus: "A Qualified Farewell" (appeared in *Antaeus* under the title "Farewell, My
Hollywood") and *English Summer, a Gothic Romance,* by Raymond Chandler, Copyright
© 1976 by Antaeus, New York, N.Y. The Atlantic Monthly: from the review by
Raymond Chandler, "The Hollywood Bowl," Copyright © 1946 by The Atlantic
Monthly Company, Boston, Mass.; reprinted with permission. Doubleday & Company,
Inc., and the Estate of W. Somerset Maugham and William Heinemann Ltd.: from *The
Summing Up* by W. Somerset Maugham, Copyright 1938 by W. Somerset Maugham;
reprinted by permission. E. P. Dutton & Co., Inc.: from *The Life of Raymond Chandler*
by Frank MacShane, Copyright © 1976 by Frank MacShane; reprinted by permission
of the publishers, E. P. Dutton & Co., Inc. Holt, Rinehart and Winston, Publishers:
from *Writing Is Work* by Mary Roberts Rinehart, which originally appeared in The
Saturday Evening Post, Copyright © 1939 by Curtis Publishing Company; reprinted
by permission of Holt, Rinehart and Winston, Publishers. Houghton Mifflin Company
and Hamish Hamilton Ltd.: from *Raymond Chandler Speaking,* edited by Dorothy
Gardiner and Kathrine Sorley Walker (1962). Hope Leresche & Sayle: from *Mr. Fortune
Objects* by H. C. Bailey. Liveright Publishing Corporation: from *Crimes of the Year* by
Joseph Gollimb. Los Angeles Times: from *Town Called Hollywood* by Philip K. Scheuer,
Copyright 1936, Los Angeles Times; reprinted by permission. The Saturday Evening
Post: from "Pickpocket Lingo," Copyright 1950. The Curtis Publishing Company;
from "Beyond Disgust," Copyright 1941, The Curtis Publishing Company; from
"Railroad Slang," Copyright 1937, The Curtis Publishing Company; all reprinted with
permission from The Saturday Evening Post. Scott Meredith Literary Agency, Inc.:
from "Some Notes on Mystery Novels and Their Authors," by Frank Gruber; reprinted
by permission of Mrs. Lois Gruber and Agents for the Estate of Frank Gruber, Scott
Meredith Literary Agency, Inc., 845 Third Avenue, New York, N.Y. 10022. The Sunday
Times (London): from "Bonded Goods" by Raymond Chandler.

Book design: Samuel N. Antupit

THE NOTEBOOKS

The Scrapbook

English Summer
illustrated by Edward Gorey

THE NOTEBOOKS OF RAYMOND CHANDLER

and

English Summer

A Gothic Romance

by

Raymond Chandler

FOREWORD

For centuries writers have recorded their thoughts and impressions in private as well as in published books. They have written diaries and journals, sometimes just to keep track of events and impressions, but also to preserve the flavor of longer periods of time and more protracted experiences. Writers have also kept notebooks as repositories of thoughts by themselves and others; they have jotted down ideas for future work, phrases, autobiographical asides, anecdotes.

The audience for such journals and notebooks is usually the writer himself, who uses them as an aid to memory and as a record of thoughts not always suitable for published work. The privacy of the diary preserves intimacy and encourages introspection. Notebooks also contain the raw material from which new works of art are made. They precede selection and are like experience itself—a lively disorder of events and impressions whose very juxtaposition can be refreshing.

Not all writers have limited their private writings to notebooks; they have kept unbound folders of notes and unpublished work and even copies of their correspondence. Raymond Chandler did all these things. During the period of twenty years that stretches from his beginnings as a pulp writer for *Black Mask* through the writing of such novels as *The Big Sleep* and *Farewell, My Lovely*, the years in Hollywood during the 1940s and his move to La Jolla, where he wrote *The Long Goodbye*, he wrote thousands of letters, many of them dictated late at night into recording machines. They are like the conversation of a lonely man too shy to have many friends to talk to.

Chandler also kept two kinds of notebook. One was a record of daily events, including notations about the progress of his work. Written by hand in small leather booklets, this first kind of notebook also contained private thoughts and observations. Over the years, these small notebooks accumulated, along with another set kept by his wife, Cissy. After her death, when Chandler was preparing to move permanently to England, he ordered that all these notebooks be taken to the San Diego dump and be destroyed.

Two black loose-leaf notebooks have survived. These are not annual diaries but are collections of miscellaneous information, mostly impersonal and literary. They include lists of similes, possible titles, story ideas, observations, drafts of articles. Most of the entries are typed, but a number appear to have been written in originally with a pencil, with Cissy typing a clear copy on top. The smaller of the two notebooks is the earlier, and, like a commonplace book, it also contains a number of passages quoted from other books as well as actual clippings from newspapers and magazines pasted in. The second notebook is larger, with lined paper and divided into sections marked Similes, Gags, Titles, Style, Notions, and Grab Bag. Much of this material is repeated from the smaller book and some of the longer entries are revised.

The first of these notebooks was begun when Chandler was starting to write seriously in the 1930s. Notations made in different pens and inks suggest that he consulted them frequently. They were like a bank where he could go when in need. During the writing of *The Little Sister*, for example, and, to a lesser extent, *The Long Goodbye*, when he was tired and often worried, he turned to the lists of similes and comparisons. If he put one in a book, he would write the initials of the book's title beside it so as not to use it a second time.

Chandler's notebooks reveal his character as a writer: he was a professional, and these are a useful working tool. At the same time, he detested pretentiousness, and sometimes, on rereading an early entry, he would pencil in "Oh, my God," or "God help us." The overall tone is good-humored, and many of the entries are funny.

The present volume also contains material that was not included in Chandler's notebooks but was preserved in his papers. The earliest was written when Chandler was a young man in England. Evidently, he took some sort of writing course, for various exercises in narrative and setting have survived, and one of them is printed here. Chandler believed that "any writer who cannot teach himself cannot be taught by others," and so after this early experience he began to follow his own advice, which was to "analyze and imitate." As a young man in England, he wrote in the manner of Saki and Henry James; in his forties in Los Angeles, he began by copying Ernest Hemingway. Included here is an unpublished parody of Hemingway written by Chandler in 1932. Moving once again to England at the end of his life, he wanted to write for the London stage. He therefore practised by writing in British English what he called alternatively "A Routine to Shock the Neighbors," and "Pornographic Sketches," two of which are printed here.

In addition to two little-known reviews, this volume also contains two other pieces of writing hitherto unpublished in book form. The first is an essay on Hollywood called "A Qualified Farewell," which was originally intended for *Screen Writer*, the journal of the Writers' Guild in Hollywood, but withdrawn by Chandler after a change of editors at the magazine. The second is a short story called "English Summer," which he originally hoped to use as the basis for a novel. Chandler preserved a warm feeling for this story throughout his life. Despite its absurdity, it reflects the sentimentality that balances the hard-boiled stance of Philip Marlowe, Chandler's fictional detective.

This collection does not include every item in the notebooks. Since the second often repeats material from the first, sometimes in a revised form, an attempt has been made to amalgamate the two. This occurs especially in "Twelve Notes on the Mystery Story." The editing has been limited to a simple reordering of the material, all of it written by Chandler.

Throughout, Chandler's spelling has been preserved, except where obvious errors occur. Punctuation, on the other hand, has been made consistent with contemporary usage. It has sometimes been necessary to guess at words, especially in hand-written passages, for Chandler's handwriting is occasionally indecipherable. All the manuscripts, including the two notebooks are from the Helga Greene Literary Agency in London. Special thanks are due Gail Rosenblum, who did much of the editorial work on this book.

Frank MacShane

THE
NOTEBOOKS
OF
RAYMOND
CHANDLER

GREAT THOUGHT

There are two kinds of truth: the truth that lights the way and the truth that warms the heart. The first of these is science, and the second is art. Neither is independent of the other or more important than the other. Without art science would be as useless as a pair of high forceps in the hands of a plumber. Without science art would become a crude mess of folklore and emotional quackery. The truth of art keeps science from becoming inhuman, and the truth of science keeps art from becoming ridiculous.

2-19-38

NOTE ON "WRITING DOWN"

from The Summing Up *by W. Somerset Maugham, Doubleday, 1938*

They (the more serious critics) told me that I had sold my soul to mammon; and the intelligentsia, of which I had been a modest but respected member, not only turned a cold shoulder on me, that would have been bad enough, but flung me, like Lucifer headlong into the bottomless pit. I was taken aback and a trifle mortified, but I bore my disgrace with fortitude, for I knew it was not the end of the story. I had desired a certain end and had taken what I thought were the only possible means to attain it; I could only shrug my shoulders if there were people so stupid as not to see that. If I had continued to write plays as bitter as *A Man of Honour* or as sardonic as *Loaves and Fishes* I should never have been given the opportunity of producing certain pieces to which not even the most severe have refused praise. The critics accused me of writing down to the public; I did not exactly do that; I had then very high spirits, a facility for amusing dialogue, an eye for a comic situation and a flippant gaiety; there was more in me than that, but this I put away for the time, and wrote my comedies with those sides of myself only that were useful to my purpose. They were designed to please and they achieved their aim.◈

[This plan for future work was typed into Chandler's notebook by his wife, Cissy. The last paragraph is clearly a note from her to him about these plans. In the years that followed, Chandler referred occasionally to this plan, and in pencil answered Cissy's question several times. He also penciled in notes in the margin of the text.]

Since all plans are foolish and those written

down are never fulfilled, let us make a plan,

this 16th. day of March 1939, at Riverside, Calif.

Got half no'. Most 1942

For the rest of 1939, all of 1940, spring of

1941, and then if there is no war and if there is

any money, to go to England for material.

Detective novels   (Law Is Where You Buy It)
Deep in Dark Water,

Based on Jade, The Man Who

Liked Dogs, Bay City Blues.

Theme, the corrupt alliance of

police and racketeers in a

small California town, outwardly

as fair as the dawn.

The Brashear Doubloon, a bur-

lesque on the pulp novelette,

with Walter and Henry. Some

stuff from Pearls are a Nuisance

but mostly new plot.

Zone of Twilight A grim witty

story of the boss politician's

son and the girl and the blending

of the upper and underworlds.

Material, Guns at Cyrano's,

Nevada Gas.

If advisable, try Goldfish for
material for a fourth.

Dramatic novel   English Summer. A short, swift,
tense, gorgeously written story
verging on melodrama, based on
my short story. The surface theme
is the American in England, the
dramatic theme is the decay of
the refined character and its
contrast with the ingenuous honest
utterly fearless and generous
American of the best type.

Short-longstories   A set of six or seven fantastic
Seven From the Stars   stories, some written, some
Seven from Nowhere.
Seven Tales from do.   thought of, perhaps one brand
new one. Each a little different
in tone and effect from the others.
The ironic gem, the Bronze Door,
the perfect fantastic atmosphere
story The Edge of the West, the
spooky story, Grandma'sboy, the
farcical story, The Disappearing
Duke, the Allegory Ironic, the
Four Gods of Bloon, The pure
fairytale The Rubies of Marmelon.

The three mystery stories should be finished in
the next two years, by end of 1940. If they make
enough for me to move to England and to forget
mystery writing and try English Summer and the
Fantastic Stories, without worrying about whether
these make money, I tackle them. But I must have two
years money ahead, and a sure market with the
detective story when I come back to it, if I do.
If English Summer is a smash hit, which it should be,
properly written, written up to the hilt but not
overwritten, I'm set for life. From then on I'll
laternate the fantastic and the dramatic until I
think of a new type. Or may do a suave detective
just for the fun.

     Dear Raymio, you'll have fun looking at
this maybe, and seeing what useless dreams you had.
Or perhaps it will not be fun.

TITLES

The Man with the Shredded Ear

All Guns Are Loaded

Choice of Dessert

Return from Ruin

Here It Is Saturday

My Best to the Bride

The Man Who Loved the Rain

The Corpse Came in Person

Law Is Where You Buy It

The Porter Rose at Dawn

We All Liked Al

Fair with Some Rain

Sit with Me While I Dream
(autobiography?)

They Only Murdered Him Once

Too Late for Smiling

The Diary of a Loud Check Suit

Deceased When Last Seen

Quick, Hide the Body

A Night in the Ice Box

Goodnight and Goodbye

The Cool-Off

The Quiet Ivories (piano used to
hide a body à la Stevenson)

Uncle Watson Wants to Think

The Parson in the Parlor

Fiction Is for Fools (article on it)

Stop Screaming—It's Me

No Third Act

Twenty Minutes' Sleep

They Still Come Honest

Between Two Liars

The Lady with the Truck

The Black-Eyed Blonde

Rigadoo (a sort of fun festival to
raise money for a worthy
purpose)

Thunder Bug (don't know what
it means?)

Islands in the Sky (anthology of
fantastic stories)

Everyone Says Good-bye Too
Soon

[Chandler's interest in titles even led him to invent a writer, Aaron Klopstein, whom he described as a suicide in Greenwich Village at the age of thirty-three. Klopstein published two novels entitled *Once More the Cicatrice* and *The Seagull Has No Friends*; two volumes of poetry, *The Hydraulic Facelift* and *Cat Hairs in the Custard*; a collection of short stories called *Twenty Inches of Monkey*—a title derived from an animal dealer's catalogue in which monkeys were advertised for vivisection at one dollar an inch; and a book of critical essays entitled *Shakespeare in Baby Talk*.

Klopstein shot himself with an Amazonian blow gun.]

Descriptive Note

Sunken gardens with a fountain at each of the
four corners. Italian garden entrance to which is
barred by a wrought iron gate with a Cupid flying
in the center. A stone seat with crouching griffins
ateach ebd. The Italian garden has busts on very
light pillars. and an oblpng podl with a large stone
water lily in it. The rose colànnade lef th the
alatr of Artemis whose lower steps overshot with
sun were visible throughbit. The inevitable sundial
made distinctive by a great corner of bright wall,
ruin of some castle keep of old days###- just distant
enough not to intercepthe declining sunlight.

(Origin unknown, found pencil-
written on scrap of paper probobbly
dating from my Redondo days. However
I wouldn't have written it down,
unless to use it.)

Used in Farewell My Lovely

JACK WOODFORD'S RULES FOR WRITING A NOVEL

Remembered from Trial and Error

1. Plan a length of 75,000 words because all publishers love to cut and 65,000 is about the right length.

2. Write a 5000 word synopsis of the action leaving out descriptive matter and character analysis and dialogue—in short everything but roughly what happens, in a major way.

3. With a blue (or possibly red) pencil, mark off where natural chapter endings may come. It is not necessary that these chapters be of equal length. It would look silly if they were. They may vary from 500 to five thousand words or even more. Nor is the number of chapters important. Thirty would be a good average, which makes an average of 2500 words to a chapter.

4. In a large loose leaf book—letter size—head up a page for each chapter with its number and an expanded (about double or treble expanded, not more) synopsis of the business allocated to that chapter. Also note the estimated number of words you are going to use for this chapter.

5. Put all these chapter pages together in a folder and at the end put a couple of pages of analysis and description of the two or three principal characters—a dossier that will make you feel you know them. Describe them physically, spiritually, and their education and background—but don't slop all over the lot and write essays.

6. In the days, weeks, or months that follow—BEFORE you actually start writing the novel—let your mind play with it bit by bit, here and there, without reference to temporal order in the story. If you think of any piece of business, character, dialogue, or in fact anything at all about any part of the story that interests you—make a note of it under the appropriate chapter.

7. The time you take on this is up to you. If you have a full mind and like the story you will soon have a full book.

8. Write the first chapter with the best opening you can think of at the moment AND LEAVE IT ALONE. If you start rewriting it and messing with it, you'll never get the book done at all. Leave it lay, brother, until the book is done.

9. Note wordage you actually use and open a shorts and overs account at the end of your loose leaf folder. In one column put words estimated for each chapter, in the next words used, and use two more columns for shorts and overs of words. This is very important indeed.

Because you have to pay back every overage before the book is half written and similarly you have to pick up every short, in expanded writing, new business, or what have you, before the book is half written. If you don't do this you will get the novel out of proportion and it will be a flop, even if you ever finish it, which you probably will not.

10. The same goes for the second half of the book.

11. If you don't know how much action it takes to fill a 75,000 word novel, synopsize a few and find out. Another way is to figure about two novelettes contain action for a full novel. This does not mean that the same number of incidents may be used and expanded as *incidents*. It means the same amount of action. In the novel there will be more transition writing, more relief writing, more playing around with dialogue and description. The actual speed of the novel should be as fast, or very nearly as fast, as the novelette, but too much story makes just as dull reading as too little story. The novel reader in general will pay some attention to how things happen and what sort of people they happen to—even if he is the same man as the novelette reader. He will have an instinctive respect for book covers that he will never give to a magazine piece, however good.

12. Don't use more than two, or at most, three main characters at first. Even very good writers get in trouble by trying to handle too many.

13. Alter your story all you please as you go along PROVIDED you don't go back and rewrite, and PROVIDED you don't stop keeping a shorts and overs account.

14. This is all there is. There isn't any more. We are talking about writing a novel—not just writing fiction. We assume you already know how to write fiction in shorter lengths. If you do, this is *all* you need to bother about to finish a novel or a hundred novels.

Note by Raymond Chandler. It should of course be born in mind that Jack Woodford can't write worth a damn on any plane BUT he probably knows plenty about how it ought to be done, if he could do it. He estimates three months as ample for a novel chore—even with other work on the side.

Further note by Raymond Chandler. The above is all bunk, in a way, although it may contain germs of truth. I paid no attention to it whatever when I wrote *The Big Sleep*.

BEYOND DISGUST

From the Saturday Evening Post, *October 1, 1941, a story by James Grant Still called "The Proud Walkers." It begins:*

◊We moved out of Houndshell mine camp in May to the homeplace father had built on Shoal Creek, and I recollect fox grapes were blooming and there was spring chill in the air. Fern and Lark and I ran ahead of the wagon, frightening water thrushes, shouting back at the poky mare mule. We broke cowcumber branches to wave at baby, wanting to call to him, but he did not then have a name. ◊

What is there about this that is beyond disgust to me? Is it the nature faking, or the fact that the attitude has been done to death so that one simply cannot feel any honesty in it? Is it that the minor cadence, the restraint, all the words, the pseudo-simplicity of the thought and so on, suggest a mind either too naïve or too phony to be endured, or a cynical imitation of something that might once have been good?

Whatever it is, it reeks.

DESCRIPTIONS OF WOMEN

From Mr. Fortune Objects *by H. C. Bailey,*
Doubleday, Doran & Company, 1938

Beside a man who was the incarnation of all the world's retired colonels sat a girl like an early Italian madonna. Not the most ethereal of them— say a Lippo Lippi madonna—not wistful, but of a simplicity of childish beauty. She was old-fashioned, or of no fashion. Her hair, which was of the madonna gold, she had drawn back smooth and flat and strained from her full, white forehead, to bind in a heavy knot above her long neck. The delicate contours of face and lip were supplied by nature. The frock, of the blue of her eyes, was plain from neck to foot and hand. She sat very still. She looked straight before her, neither shy nor asking notice, not ill at ease but as if she found them all strange people.

A girl with whom pains had been taken. Her thin, bare arms had a marble sheen; some of the shape of her slim body was displayed, the rest concealed in a froth of filmy frills, the same colour as her turquoise eyes, which invited attention to the concentration of art on her head. The lips, the complexion, had the emphasis of a magazine cover; the eyebrows were orange lines. A little blue hat was cocked askew, to show that her flaxen hair had been cropped short and put into tight poodle curls. She smiled and smiled.

FASHION NOTES — MEN

1. Gazelle leather sports coat nutmeg brown
2. Coconut straw hat deep beige with pugaree band
3. Light tweed jacket with dark buttons, plaid slacks, alligator shoes, soft brown shirt, narrow bow tie, brown felt hat with narrow snap brim
4. Creamy white shetland wool sports coat with dark Oxford gray slacks, solid burgundy four-in-hand tie, plaided handkerchief to match, plain white shirt and tie. Collar slightly stiffened.

Oh my God.

May 16, 1937

STORY IDEA: FANTASTIC

Title—Bingo's Snuff

A variation on the old invisibility idea. A middle-aged Caspar Milque-toast kind of man is much embarrassed and humiliated by constantly walking in on love scenes between his wife and her boyfriend. He wishes he could be invisible when he does it, to spare them and himself, not to spy on them.

One day he looks out of the window and sees a peculiar looking elderly party passing the house. The party turns up the walk and the doorbell rings. Hero answers the door. Elderly party hands him a card advertising Bingo's Snuff, waits for him to read it, nods and walks down the steps, stops to take a pinch of snuff, and instantly disappears. Later reappears further down the street, politely lifts his hat to hero, and goes away.

Hero goes to address on the card, finds the same elderly party behind desk. Business discussion about the snuff, demonstration by elderly party, and hero finally buys some. Various idiotic complications from here on, possibly ending in affair with police trying to arrest Bingo while he is in his office invisible, occasionally opening the door to kick a policeman in the stomach.

6-3-43

He was a man who liked to make small neat inconspicuous motions with his hands. These motions neither had, nor were intended to have, any meaning. But the making of them gave him a quiet sense of his own grace and competence.

NARRATION

[Exercise written for Short Story Writing 52AB, received a grade of "A."]

One-eyed Mellow glanced at the braid, once no doubt gold, that adorned the outer edges of his sleeves. He smiled insidiously, and his hand, with a movement very familiar to his men, began to wander towards the pistol stuck in his sash. As he freed it, coolly and without haste, from the broad band of dirty silk, the little dark sailor made an abrupt but very graceful movement. One-eyed Mellow's glance turned rapidly to the wall at his elbow, and he perceived his pistol hanging by the trigger-guard on the blade of a slim dagger.

"Very pretty," he drawled at length, when the silence threatened to become unbearable. "Very pretty work indeed." His Adam's-apple moved restlessly under the skin of his lean throat.

The little dark sailor slipped around the head of the table and plucked his dagger from the wall.

"Your pistol, I believe, Captain," he remarked in a mincing tone, and politely held out the weapon to its owner.

"Thank 'ee, my man," said One-eyed Mellow, a little wearily.

IN DEFENSE OF THE CLASSICS

Extract from page 17 of the original first issue of Time, *reprinted with February 28, 1938 issue*

There is however an argument for the retention of the classics as compulsory subjects of education which cannot be ignored. It is the argument that the classics have now been taught so long that they cannot be dropped. It does not rest upon the respective glories and grandeurs of Athens and Rome. It rests merely upon the fact that Greek and Roman thinking is the core of our culture; that without the literatures of these two tongues we are without an understanding of our traditions; that cut off from our traditions, we are novices where we should be adepts.

If the great universities, with their manifold departments, and courses, and degrees, retain no common courses in any way related to the history of the race, they will graduate men and women who will have nothing in common but their clothes. They will not even talk the same tongue, though they may all speak a dialect of one language. They will be free and unrestrained individuals. And they will have no ancestors whatever.

BEGINNING OF AN ESSAY

The keynote of American civilization is a sort of warm-hearted vulgarity. The Americans have none of the irony of the English, none of their cool poise, none of their manner. But they do have friendliness. Where an Englishman would give you his card, an American would very likely give you his shirt.

NOTES (VERY BRIEF, PLEASE) ON ENGLISH AND AMERICAN STYLE

The merits of American style are less numerous than its defects and annoyances, but they are more powerful.

It is a fluid language, like Shakespearean English, and easily takes in new words, new meanings for old words, and borrows at will and at ease from the usages of other languages, for example, the German free compounding of words and the use of noun or adjective as verb; the French simplification of grammar, the use of one, he, etc.

Its overtones and undertones are not stylized into a social conventional kind of subtlety which is in effect a class language. If they exist at all, they have a real impact.

It is more alive to clichés. Consider the appalling, because apparently unconscious, use of clichés by as good a writer as Maugham in *The Summing Up*, the deadly repetition of pet words until they almost make you scream. And the pet words are always little half-archaic words like *jejune* and *umbrage* and *vouchsafe*, none of which the average educated person could even define correctly.

Its impact is sensational rather than intellectual. It expresses things experienced rather than ideas.

It is a mass language only in the same sense that its baseball slang is born of baseball players. That is, it is a language which is being molded by writers to do delicate things and yet be within the grasp of superficially educated people. It is not a natural growth, much as its proletarian writers would like to think so. But compared with it at its best, English has reached the Alexandrian stage of formalism and decay.

It has Disadvantages.

It overworks its catchphrases until they not merely become meaningless playtalk, like English catchphrases, but sickening, like overworked popular songs.

Its slang, being invented by writers and palmed off on simple hoodlums and ballplayers, often has a phony sound, even when fresh.

The language has no awareness of the continuing stream of culture. This may or may not be due to the collapse of classical education and it may or may not happen also in English. It is certainly due to a lack of the historical sense and to shoddy education, because American is an ill-at-ease language, without manner or self-control.

It has too great a fondness for the *faux naïf*, by which I mean the use of a style such as might be spoken by a very limited sort of mind. In the hands of a genius like Hemingway this may be effective, but only by subtly evading the terms of the contract, that is, by an artistic use of the telling detail which the speaker never would have noted. When not used by a genius it is as flat as a Rotarian speech.

The last noted item is very probably the result of the submerged but still very strong homespun revolt against English cultural superiority. "We're just as good as they are, even if we don't talk good grammar." This attitude is based on complete ignorance of the English people as a mass. Very few of them talk good grammar. Those that do probably speak more correctly than the same type of American, but the homespun Englishman uses as much bad grammar as the American, some of it being as old as *Piers Ploughman*, but still bad grammar. But you don't hear English professional men making elementary mistakes in the use of their own language. You do hear that constantly in America. Of course anyone who likes can put up an argument against any other person's ideas of correctness. Naturally this is historical up to a point and contemporary up to a point. There must be some compromise, or we should all be Alexandrians or boors. But roughly and ordinarily and plainly speaking, you hear American doctors and lawyers and school-masters talking in such a way that it is very clear they have no real understanding of their own language and its good or bad form. I'm not referring to the deliberate use of slang and colloquialisms; I'm referring to the pathetic attempts of such people to speak with unwonted correctness and horribly failing.

You don't hear this sort of collapse of grammar in England among the same kind of people.

It's fairly obvious that American education is a cultural flop. Americans are not a well-educated people culturally, and their vocational education often has to be learned all over again after they leave school and college. On the other hand they have open quick minds and if their education has little sharp positive value, it has not the stultifying effects of a more rigid training. Such tradition as they have in the use of their language is derived from English tradition, and there is just enough resentment about this to cause perverse use of ungrammaticalities—"just to show 'em."

Americans, having the most complex civilization the world has seen, still like to think of themselves as plain people. In other words they like to think the comic-strip artist is a better draftsman than Leonardo— just because he is a comic-strip artist and the comic strip is for plain people.

American style has no cadence. Without cadence a style has no harmonics. It is like a flute playing solo, an incomplete thing, very dexterous or very stupid as the case may be, but still an incomplete thing.

Since political power still dominates culture, American will dominate English for a long time to come. English, being on the defensive, is static and cannot contribute anything but a sort of waspish criticism of forms and manners. America is a land of mass production which has only just reached the concept of quality. Its style is utilitarian and essentially vulgar. Why then can it produce great writing or, at any rate, writing as great as this age is likely to produce? The answer is, it can't. All the best American writing has been done by men who are, or at some time were, cosmopolitans. They found here a certain freedom of expression, a certain richness of vocabulary, a certain wideness of interest. But they had to have European taste to use the material.

Final note—out of order— The tone quality of English speech is usually overlooked. This tone quality is infinitely variable and contributes infinite meaning. The American voice is flat, toneless, and tiresome. The English tone quality makes a thinner vocabulary and a more formalized use of language capable of infinite meanings. Its tones are of course read into written speech by association. This makes good English a class language, and that is its fatal defect. The English writer is a gentleman (or not a gentleman) first and a writer second.

BEER IN THE SERGEANT MAJOR'S HAT (OR THE SUN ALSO SNEEZES)

*Dedicated with no good reason to the greatest living American novelist
—Ernest Hemingway*

Hank went into the bathroom to brush his teeth.

"The hell with it," he said. "She shouldn't have done it."

It was a good bathroom. It was small and the green enamel was peeling off the walls. But the hell with that, as Napoleon said when they told him Josephine waited without. The bathroom had a wide window through which Hank looked at the pines and larches. They dripped with a faint rain. They looked smooth and comfortable.

"The hell with it," Hank said. "She shouldn't have done it."

He opened the cabinet over the washbasin and took out his toothpaste. He looked at his teeth in the mirror. They were large yellow teeth, but sound. Hank could still bite his way for a while.

Hank unscrewed the top of the toothpaste tube, thinking of the day when he had unscrewed the lid of the coffee jar, down on the Pukayuk River, when he was trout fishing. There had been larches there too. It was a damn good river, and the trout had been damn good trout. They liked being hooked. Everything had been good except the coffee, which had been lousy. He had made it Watson's way, boiling it for two hours and a half in his knapsack. It had tasted like hell. It had tasted like the socks of the Forgotten Man.

"She shouldn't have done it," Hank said out loud. Then he was silent.

Hank put the toothpaste down and looked around. There was a bottle of alcohol on top of the built-in drawers where the towels were kept. It was grain alcohol. Velma hated rubbing alcohol with its harsh irritants. Her skin was sensitive. She hated almost everything. That was because she was sensitive. Hank picked up the bottle of alcohol, pulled the cork out, and smelled it. It had a damn good smell. He poured some alcohol into his tooth glass and added some water. Then the alcohol was all misty, with little moving lines in it, like tiny ripples coming to the surface. Only they didn't come to the surface. They just stayed in the alcohol, like goldfish in a bowl.

Hank drank the alcohol and water. It had a warm sweetish taste.

It was warm all the way down. It was warm as hell. It was warmer than whiskey. It was warmer than that Asti Spumante they had that time in Capozzo when Hank was with the Arditi. They had been carp fishing with landing nets. It had been a good day. After the fourth bottle of Asti Spumante Hank fell into the river and came out with his hair full of carp. Old Peguzzi laughed until his boots rattled on the hard gray rock. And afterward Peguzzi got gonorrhea on the Piave. It was a hell of a war.

Hank poured more alcohol into the glass and added less water. He drank solemnly, liking his face in the mirror. It was warm and a bit shiny. His eyes had a kind of fat glitter. They were large pale blue eyes, except when he was mad. Then they were dark blue. When he had a good edge on they were almost gray. They were damn good eyes.

"The hell with it," he said. "She shouldn't have done it."

He poured more alcohol into the glass and added a little water—very little. He raised the glass in a toast to his face in the mirror.

"Gentlemen, I give you alcohol. Not, gentlemen, because I cannot give you wine or whiskey, but because I desire to cultivate in you the fundamental art of intoxication. The alcohol drinker, gentlemen, is the hair-shirt drinker. He likes his penance strong."

Hank drained the glass and refilled it. The bottle was nearly empty now, but there was more alcohol in the cellar. It was a good cellar, and there was plenty of alcohol in it.

"Gentlemen," Hank said, "when I was with Napoleon at Solferino we drank cognac. When I was with Moore at Coruña we drank port with a dash of brandy. It was damn good port, and Moore was a damn good drinker. When I was with Kitchener at Khartoum we drank the stale of horses. With Kuroki on the Yalu I drank saki, and with Byng at Arras I drank Scotch. These, gentlemen, were drinks of diverse charms. Now that I am with you, gentlemen, we shall drink alcohol, because alcohol is the Holy Mother of all drinking."

Hank's face in the mirror wavered like a face behind thin smoke. It was a face drawn on gray silk by unscrupulous shadows. It was not a face at all. Hank scowled at it. The reflected scowl was as merciless as an earthquake.

"The hell with it," he said. "She shouldn't have done it."

He leaned against the washbowl and squeezed some toothpaste on his toothbrush. It was a long toothbrush, about six feet long. It was springy, like a trout rod. Hank brought his elbow around with a sweep and spread some toothpaste on his upper lip. He supported himself with both hands and squinted at his reflection.

"The white mustache, gentlemen," he burbled. "The mark of a goddamn ambassador."

Hank drank the rest of the alcohol straight. For a moment his stomach came up between his ears. But that passed and he only felt as if he had been bitten in the back of the neck by a tiger.

"Not by a damn sight she shouldn't," he said.

With large gestures he applied toothpaste to his eyebrows and temples.

"Not a complete work, gentlemen," he yelled. "Just an indication of what can be done. And now for a brief moment I leave you. While I am gone let your conversation be clean."

Hank stumbled down to the living room. It seemed a long way to the cellar where the alcohol was. There were steps to go down. The hell with the steps.

The cat was sleeping in a tight curve on the carpet.

"Jeeze Christ," Hank said. "'At's a hell of a fine cat."

It was a large black cat with long fur. It was a cat a guy could get on with. Jeeze Christ, yes. Hank lay down on the floor and put his head on the cat. The cat licked at the toothpaste on Hank's eyebrow. Then it sneezed and bit his ear.

"Jeeze Christ," Hank said. "The hell with it. She shouldn't have done it."

He slept.

Aug. 7th, 1932

A ROUTINE
TO SHOCK THE
NEIGHBOURS:
IS IT ANY WONDER?

Note: The monologue of a third-rate British film star addressed to a friend, male or female, the idea being an attempt to write a certain sort of British English.

Darling—

Well, darling, I'm sure you must know by this time. There was this absolute horror called a film script—that is what they called the beastly thing at any rate—no story, no plot, some concoction by some awful person named Chandler, and, darling, positively not five lines to a page for me. And God, what dialogue! I mean, absolutely horrible lines such as "Good evening, Lord Tinwoody, so delighted you could come." I ask you, darling, just what can one *do* with lines like that? Except possibly smoke a rather nasty briar pipe.

Well, here we were at Welwyn or Welford or something and this complete idiot of a director fussing around as though the whole thing wasn't obviously a nonsense. . . . No, I absolutely refuse to speak to anyone on the telephone. I'm creating a role. . . . Oh well, do you want me to have laryngitis or something and lose the part? . . . I quite agree, it couldn't be more revolting. . . . Why not then go somewhere else and be an agent? They say South America . . . Sorry, darling. Then this atrociously handsome silver-haired but so young American officer was brought around just to have a sort of look at the beastly place in a beastly sort of way.

I was adjusting my nylons and when I adjust a nylon I really adjust a nylon. He looked at me in some small embarrassment. I flashed him a smile. But some horrible publicity beetle began to drag him away when Tony managed to stop all that. . . . Tony? Darling, I haven't a clue, but he does seem to do things. . . . Oh, I suppose so. One rather has to occasionally with all these people, but I don't remember. I imagine it was average, but not distinguished. Then suddenly there was this American with his silver eagles—they call them bird colonels, you know —and I was still adjusting my nylons. He smiled rather bashfully. I expect you know what he was looking at. After all, men do, rather.

Somebody said: "Miss Sprindrift, may I present Colonel Elmer Lynwood?"

He had a really darling smile, but what is this Elmer business? Is that a name or something? At any rate he kissed my hand in a rather obscure continental style and said he was pleased to meet me. Well—if you call that sort of thing meeting a person. At any rate I smiled quite brilliantly. He asked me how I liked being in the movies.

"In what?"

"Oh, I beg your pardon if I said the wrong thing. You call them films or cinema or something, I believe."

"Not this trash. One merely turns one's head away to escape the fumes of decomposition."

"I guess I'm all balled up," he said. "I thought there was some kind of a movie being shot here and that you were the star. You were introduced to me as Miss Delphine Sprindrift, weren't you?"

"You were introduced to me," I said. "Otherwise *on y est*, whatever that means."

"I'm sorry. That one went clear over the centerfield wall."

I hadn't the remotest now. But he did seem like someone one wouldn't positively abhor. I gave him my melting smile. Rather nice, too.

"Are you about to shoot a scene, Miss Sprindrift? I'd love to watch."

"Not if I remain conscious," I said. "Let's drift off to my flat and have a drink."

"Oh, do you think we could get away with it? After all they are making a movie."

"Don't worry," I said. "They may think so, but I know they are just making idiots of themselves."

Well, darling, to make a long story slightly shorter, we did drive out to the flat in one of those command cars they have, or perhaps staff cars is the word, but with one of the wonderful, wonderful American chauffeurs who drive as if they were in bed with a woman—always with such absolute perfection and skill—they just throw it away they have so much of it—and it just occurred to me—well, there was this darling American colonel and the electric fire—one always thinks Americans are cold, but their climate . . . Well, the hell with that, but if you mention central heating to me again I shall most positively scream!

He mixed a couple of absolutely adorable martinis and I sipped mine in the most available manner. But he hadn't a clue, not a trace.

I adjusted my nylons again. Reaction negative.

"Are you too warm, Colonel?" I asked.

He smiled with that bloody awful American politeness. I could see that he was perspiring, but he would never have admitted it, so he said he was quite comfortable.

"Can I mix you another drink before I leave?" he asked.

"That would be divine," I said.

He went over to the bar thing in the corner, and the moment his back was turned I stripped and lay on the couch in the most abandoned manner.

He turned with a glass in each hand.

"Oh dear, I have a wife in Sioux City," he said mournfully.

"A squaw?"

"Oh no, it's not Indians any more. Hasn't been for a long time. But I really think I must go now. I hope we get together again sometime."

He put the two glasses on the piano.

"Drop dead in Birmingham," I said.

"I beg your pardon."

"Skip it," I said, crossing my legs as gracefully as one can when nude. "Sioux City, huh? You should live so long, Colonel. Well, nuts to everything, as we say in Grosvenor Square."

He put his blue Air Force cap on and saluted me. That really dislodged me. "I had no idea you were an American," he said apologetically, "but I do have this lovely wife in Sioux City, and I really thank you for your hospitality."

Then the bastard stood there and saluted me again, darling, and I hadn't a stitch, but not a stitch.

I said: "I'm not an American. God be thanked for that. I'm merely a woman who was ready to be taken by anyone with an ounce of guts. Does that answer your stupid silly Sioux City question? Thank you for nothing, and more especially for putting wet glasses on my piano. We are not so terribly rich over here, you know. It sometimes takes a long long time to earn enough money to refinish a grand piano. Far more than the cost of four rows of ribbons and an American officer's set of suntans. Nice to have met you, Colonel. And now goodbye."

He left, but he removed the glasses, which in a way was rather sweet. I heard the lovely car leaving. I thought possibly the lovely driver might come back. But he didn't. So there you are, darling. Is it any wonder?

THE END

LINES TO A LADY WITH AN UNSPLIT INFINITIVE

[When the galleys for one of Chandler's articles in the *Atlantic Monthly* were returned for his corrections, he noticed that certain changes had been made in his text. Accordingly, he wrote as follows to Edward Weeks, the *Atlantic*'s editor: "Would you convey my compliments to the purist who reads your proofs and tell him or her that I write a sort of broken-down patois which is something like the way a Swiss waiter talks, and that when I split an infinitive, God damn it, I split it so it will stay split, and when I interrupt the velvety smoothness of my more or less literate syntax with a few sudden words of bar-room vernacular, that is done with the eyes wide open and the mind relaxed but attentive." Chandler's letter so delighted Weeks he showed it to the proofreader in question, Miss Margaret Mutch, whose name later inspired Chandler's verses as printed below.]

Miss Margaret Mutch she raised her crutch
    With a wild Bostonian cry.
"Though you went to Yale, your grammar is frail,"
    She snarled as she jabbed his eye.
"Though you went to Princeton I never winced on
    Such a horrible relative clause!
Though you went to Harvard no decent larva'd
    Accept your syntactical flaws.
Taught not to drool at a Public School
    (With a capital P and S)
You are drooling still with your shall and will
    You're a very disgusting mess!"

She jabbed his eye with a savage cry.
    She laughed at his anguished shrieks.
O'er the Common he fled with a hole in his head.
    To heal it took Weeks and Weeks.

"O dear Miss Mutch, don't raise your crutch
        To splinter my new glass eye!
There ain't no school that can teach a fool
        The whom of the me and the I.
There ain't no grammar that equals a hammer
        To nail down a cut-rate wit.
And the verb 'to be' as employed by me
        Is often and lightly split.
A lot of my style (so-called) is vile,
        For I learned to write in a bar.
The marriage of thought to words was wrought
        With many a strong sidecar.
A lot of my stuff is extremely rough,
        For I had no maiden aunts.
O dear Miss Mutch, leave go your clutch
        On Noah Webster's pants!

"The grammarian will, when the poet lies still,
        Instruct him in how to sing.
The rules are clean; they are right, I ween,
        But where do they make the *thing*?
In the waxy gloam of a Funeral Home
        Where the gray morticians bow?
Is it written best on a palimpsest,
        Or carved on a whaleboat's prow?
Is it neatly joint with needlepoint
        To the chair that was Grandma's pride?
Or smeared in blood on the shattered wood
        Where the angry rebel died?

"O dear Miss Mutch, put down your crutch,
        And leave us crack a bottle.
A guy like I weren't meant to die
        On the grave of Aristotle.
O leave us dance on the dead romance
        Of the small but clear footnote.
The infinitive with my fresh-honed shiv
        I will split from heel to throat.
Roll on, roll on, thou semicolon,
        Ye commas crisp and brown.
The apostrophe will stretch like toffee
        When we nail the full stop down.
Oh, hand in hand with the ampersand
        We'll tread a measure brisk.

We'll stroll all night by the delicate light
        Of a well-placed asterisk.
As gay as a lark in the fragrant dark
        We'll hoist and down the tipple.
With laughter light we'll greet the plight
        Of the hanging participle!"

She stared him down with an icy frown.
        His accidence she shivered.
His face was white with sudden fright,
        His syntax lily-livered.
"O dear Miss Mutch, leave down your crutch!"
        He cried in thoughtless terror.
Short shrift she gave. Above his grave:
        HERE LIES A PRINTER'S ERROR.

A DEFENSE OF IMPURITY TAKEN FROM *SOUTH WIND*, BY NORMAN DOUGLAS

Page 105, Hampton Court Edition, Sun Dial Press, 1938

[Chandler's additions are in brackets.]

You exalt purity to a bad eminence, Keith would remark. What did you say about the book I lent you the other day? you said it was morbid and indecent; you said that no clean-minded person would care to read it. And yet, after an unnecessary amount of arguing, you were forced to admit that the subject was interesting and that the writer dealt with it in an interesting manner. What more can you expect from an author? Believe me, this hankering after purity, this hypersensitiveness as to what is morbid or immoral, is by no means a good sign. A healthy man refuses to be hampered by preconceived notions of what is wrong or ugly. When he reads a book like that he either yawns or laughs. That is because he is sure of himself. I could give you a long list of celebrated statesmen, princes, philosophers and prelates of the Church who take pleasure, in their moments of relaxation, in what you would call improper conversation, literature or correspondence. They feel the strain of being continually pure; they realize that all strains are pernicious, and that there is no action without its reaction. They unbend. Only invertebrate folks do not unbend. They dare not, because they have no backbone. They know that if they once unbent, they could not straighten themselves out again. They make a virtue of their own organic defect. They explain their natural imperfection by calling themselves pure. . . . [A pure man is a poor man and] a poor man is a wintry tree—alive, but stripped of its shining splendor. He is always denying himself this or that. One by one, his humane instincts, his elegant desires, are starved away by stress of circumstance. The charming diversity of life ceases to have any meaning for him. To console himself, he sets up perverse canons of right and wrong. What the rich do, that is wrong. Why? Because he does not do it. Why not? Because he has no money. A poor man [and a pure man] is forced into a hypocritical attitude towards life—debarred from being intellectually honest. He cannot pay for the necessary experience.

SOME NOTES ON MYSTERY NOVELS AND THEIR AUTHORS
BY FRANK GRUBER

[Frank Gruber is the author of "Mask of Dimitrios" and the Johnny Fletcher and Simon Lash mystery series. Place of publication unknown; approximate date, 1940s.]

Edgar Allan Poe invented the detective story, back in 1841. His M. Dupin, "Murders in the Rue Morgue," was the grandfather of all fictional detectives. In 1867 came Wilkie Collins with *The Moonstone* and Sergeant Cuff. In 1888 A. Conan Doyle patterned his Sherlock Holmes after Poe's M. Dupin and brought the detective story to maturity and worldwide popularity.

The first successful book-length detective novel published in the United States was *The Leavenworth Case* (1876). It was written by Anna Katharine Green and is still being read today. *The Circular Staircase*, by Mary Roberts Rinehart, was published in 1908 and has sold more than 3,000,000 copies to date. A cheap edition was brought out only two years ago.

In the 1920s S. S. Van Dine brought the detective story into the drawing room and reached the 100,000 mark in book sales. Dashiell Hammett originated the "tough" school of detective stories. *The Maltese Falcon*, considered by many critics to be the best detective story of modern times, was published serially in a pulp magazine, *Black Mask*. Hammett followed *The Maltese Falcon* with *The Thin Man* in 1932 and hasn't written another detective story since, although he could write his own publishing contract.

The average mystery novel sells less than 2500 copies; between 15 and 20 of every year's offerings sell from 5000 to 10,000 copies and a meager six or eight more than 10,000. These figures pertain to the regular $2 editions only, for the better-selling authors are also published in larger, cheaper editions. The Grosset & Dunlap editions which sell for $1 (raised from 75 cents) run from 5000 to 10,000 copies. Then come the 49 cent editions in from 10,000 to 20,000 copies. And finally the 25 cent pocket books, ranging from 100,000 to 200,000 copies per title. The Detective Book club takes on 36 mystery titles a year and may bring another 100,000 circulation. A best selling mystery novel, therefore, may have approximately 350,000 circulation.

This is exclusive of magazine and newspaper serialization. *The French Key* was published serially in a magazine before book publication and, after book publication, was syndicated to more than 30 newspapers with a total circulation of 10,000,000.

Most of the better mysteries are also published in Great Britain and South America and, before the war, in France and other European democracies. The dictatorships banned mysteries a decade ago.

Modern detective stories fall into seven loose classifications: (1) the deductive story (clues and deducing), (2) the tough school (gore, sex and four-letter words), (3) the had-I-but-known, (4) the old maid schoolteacher detective (the lace panties story), (5) the locked-room murder method, (6) the fast-action thriller, (7) the screwball, anything goes story.

About 150 mystery novels were published during the past year. Before the war 300 mysteries were published every year. The sharp decline in the quantity of this product is due to three causes: (1) paper shortage, (2) the army, navy and OWI have taken some of the mystery writers, (3) Frank Gruber gave up writing mystery novels and came to Hollywood.

Personal nominations for the 10 best mystery writers of today are: (1) Frank Gruber (naturally), (2) Erle Stanley Gardner, (3) Raymond Chandler, (4) Georges Simenon (translated from the French), (5) Arthur W. Upfield (Australian), (6) Agatha Christie, (7) Ellery Queen (two guys named Fred Dannay and Manfred Lee), (8) Dorothy B. Hughes, (9) Mignon Eberhart, (10) I can't think of the 10th.

I have an unlisted telephone number; I own a large, vicious dog and have already placed an order for a set of brass knuckles. So, if I've left your name off this list of "10 best," just drop me a postcard in care of the dead letter office.◈

TWELVE NOTES
ON THE MYSTERY STORY

1. It must be credibly motivated, both as to the original situation and the denouement; it must consist of the plausible actions of plausible people in plausible circumstances, it being remembered that plausibility is largely a matter of style. This requirement rules out most trick endings and a great many "closed circle" stories in which the least likely character is forcibly made over into the criminal, without convincing anybody. It also rules out such elaborate mises-en-scène as Christie's *Murder in a Calais Coach*, where the whole setup for the crime requires such a fluky set of happenings that it could never seem real.

2. It must be technically sound as to the methods of murder and detection. No fantastic poisons or improper effects from poison such as death from nonfatal doses, etc. No use of silencers on revolvers (they won't work) or snakes climbing bellropes ("The Speckled Band"). Such things at once destroy the foundation of the story. If the detective is a trained policeman, he must act like one, and have the mental and physical equipment that go with the job. If he is a private investigator or amateur, he must at least know enough about police methods not to make an ass of himself. When a policeman is made out to be a fool, as he always was in the Sherlock Holmes stories, this not only deprecates the accomplishment of the detective but it makes the reader doubt the author's knowledge of his own field. Conan Doyle and Poe were primitives in this art and stand in relation to the best modern writers as Giotto does to da Vinci. They did things which are no longer permissible and exposed ignorances that are no longer tolerated. Also, police art, itself, was rudimentary in their time. "The Purloined Letter" would not fool a modern cop for four minutes. Conan Doyle showed no knowledge whatever of the organization of Scotland Yard's men. Christie commits the same stupidities in our time, but that doesn't make them right. Contrast Austin Freeman, who wrote a story about a forged fingerprint ten years before police method realized such things could be done.

3. It must be honest with the reader. This is always said, but the implications are not realized. Important facts not only must not be concealed, they must not be distorted by false emphasis. Unimportant facts must not be projected in such a way as to make them portentous. (This creation of red herrings and false menace out of trick camera work and mood shots is the typical Hollywood mystery picture cheat.) Inferences from the facts are the detective's stock in trade; but he

should disclose enough to keep the reader's mind working. It is arguable, although not certain, that inferences arising from special knowledge (e.g., Dr. Thorndyke) are a bit of a cheat, because the basic theory of all good mystery writing is that at some stage not too late in the story the reader did have the materials to solve the problem. If special scientific knowledge was necessary to interpret the facts, the reader did not have the solution unless he had the special knowledge. It may have been Austin Freeman's feeling about this that led him to the invention of the inverted detective story, in which the reader knows the solution from the beginning and takes his pleasure from watching the detective trace it out a step at a time.

4. It must be realistic as to character, setting, and atmosphere. It must be about real people in a real world. Very few mystery writers have any talent for character work, but that doesn't mean it is not necessary. It makes the difference between the story you reread and remember and the one you skim through and almost instantly forget. Those like Valentine Williams who say the problem overrides everything are merely trying to cover up their own inability to create character.

5. It must have a sound story value apart from the mystery element; i.e., the investigation itself must be an adventure worth reading.

6. To achieve this it must have some form of suspense, even if only intellectual. This does not mean menace and especially it does not mean that the detective must be menaced by grave personal danger. This last is a trend and like all trends will exhaust itself by overimitation. Nor need the reader be kept hanging onto the edge of his chair. The overplotted story can be dull too; too much shock may result in numbness to shock. But there must be conflict, physical, ethical or emotional, and there must be some element of danger in the broadest sense of the word.

7. It must have color, lift, and a reasonable amount of dash. It takes an awful lot of technical adroitness to compensate for a dull style, although it has been done, especially in England.

8. It must have enough essential simplicity to be explained easily when the times comes. (This is possibly the most often violated of all the rules). The ideal denouement is one in which everything is revealed in a flash of action. This is rare because ideas that good are always rare. The explanation need not be very short (except on the screen), and often it cannot be short; but it must be interesting in itself, it must be something the reader is anxious to hear, and not a new story with a new set of characters, dragged in to justify an overcomplicated plot. Above all the explanation must not be merely a long-winded assembling of minute circumstances which no ordinary reader could possibly be expected to remember. To make the solution dependent on this is a kind of unfair-

ness, since here again the reader did not have the solution within his grasp, in any practical sense. To expect him to remember a thousand trivialities and from them to select that three that are decisive is as unfair as to expect him to have a profound knowledge of chemistry, metallurgy, or the mating habits of the Patagonian anteater.

9. It must baffle a reasonably intelligent reader. This opens up a very difficult question. Some of the best detective stories ever written (those of Austin Freeman, for example) seldom baffle an intelligent reader to the end. But the reader does not guess the *complete solution* and could not himself have made a logical demonstration of it. Since readers are of many minds, some will guess a cleverly hidden murder and some will be fooled by the most transparent plot. (Could "The Red-Headed League" ever really fool a modern reader?) It is not necessary or even possible to fool to the hilt the real aficionado of mystery fiction. A mystery story that consistently did that and was honest would be unintelligible to the average fan; he simply would not know what the story was all about. But there must be some important elements of the story that elude the most penetrating reader.

10. The solution must seem inevitable once revealed. This is the least often emphasized element of a good mystery, but it is one of the important elements of all fiction. It is not enough merely to fool or elude or sidestep the reader; you must make him feel that he ought not to have been fooled and that the fooling was honorable.

11. It must not try to do everything at once. If it is a puzzle story operating in a rather cool, reasonable atmosphere, it cannot also be a violent adventure or a passionate romance. An atmosphere of terror destroys logical thinking; if the story is about the intricate psychological pressures that lead apparently ordinary people to commit murder, it cannot then switch to the cool analysis of the police investigator. The detective cannot be hero and menace at the same time; the murderer cannot be a tormented victim of circumstance and also a heavy.

12. It must punish the criminal in one way or another, not necessarily by operation of the law. Contrary to popular (and Johnston Office) belief, this requirement has nothing much to do with morality. It is a part of the logic of detection. If the detective fails to resolve the consequences of the crime, the story is an unresolved chord and leaves irritation behind it.

Addenda

---

1. The perfect detective story cannot be written. The type of mind which can evolve the perfect problem is not the type of mind that

can produce the artistic job of writing. It would be nice to have Dashiell Hammett and Austin Freeman in the same book, but it just isn't possible. Hammett couldn't have the plodding patience and Freeman couldn't have the verve for narrative. They don't go together. Even a fair compromise such as Dorothy Sayers is less satisfying than the two types taken separately.

2. The most effective way to conceal a simple mystery is behind another mystery. This is literary legerdemain. You do not fool the reader by hiding clues or faking character à la Christie but by making him solve the wrong problem.

3. It has been said that "nobody cares about the corpse." This is bunk. It is throwing away a valuable element. It is like saying the murder of your aunt means no more to you than the murder of an unknown man in an unknown part of a city you never visited.

4. Flip dialogue is not wit.

5. A mystery serial does not make a good mystery novel. The "curtains" depend for their effect on your not having the next chapter to read at once. In book form these curtains give the effect of a false suspense and tend to be merely irritating. The magazines have begun to find that out.

6. Love interest nearly always weakens a mystery story because it creates a type of suspense that is antagonistic and not complementary to the detective's struggle to solve the problem. The kind of love interest that works is the one that complicates the problem by adding to the detective's troubles but which at the same time you instinctively feel will not survive the story. A really good detective never gets married. He would lose his detachment, and this detachment is part of his charm.

7. The fact that love interest is played up in the big magazines and on the screen doesn't make it artistic. Women are supposed to be the targets of magazine fiction and movies. The magazines are not interested in mystery writing as an art. They are not interested in any kind of writing as an art.

8. The hero of the mystery story is the detective. Everything hangs on his personality. If he hasn't one, you have very little. And you have *very few* really good mystery stories. Naturally.

9. The criminal cannot be the detective. This is an old rule and has once in a while been violated successfully, but it is sound as it ever was. For this reason: the detective by tradition and definition is the seeker after truth. He can't be that if he already knows the truth. There is an implied guarantee to the reader that the detective is on the level.

10. The same remark applies to the story where the first-person narrator is the criminal. I should personally have to qualify this by saying that for me the first-person narration can always be accused of subtle dishonesty because of its appearance of candor and its ability to

suppress the detective's ratiocination while giving a clear account of his words and acts. Which opens up the much larger question of what honesty really is in this context; is it not a matter of degree rather than an absolute? I think it is and always will be. Regardless of the candor of the first-person narrative there comes a time when the detective has made up his mind and yet does not communicate this to the reader. He holds some of his thinking out for the denouement or explanation. He tells the facts but not the reaction in his mind to those facts. Is this a permissible convention of deceit? It must be; otherwise the detective telling his own story could not have solved the problem in advance of the technical denouement. Once in a lifetime a story such as *The Big Sleep* holds almost nothing back; the denouement is an action which the reader meets as soon as the detective. The theorizing from that action follows immediately. There is only a momentary concealment of the fact that Marlowe loaded the gun with blanks when he gave it to Carmen down by the oil sump. But even this is tipped off to the reader when he says, "If she missed the can, which she was certain to do, she would probably hit the wheel. That would stop a small slug completely. However she wasn't going to hit even that." He doesn't say why, but the action follows so quickly that you don't feel any real concealment.

11. The murderer must not be a loony. The murderer is not a murderer unless he commits murder in the legal sense.

12. There is, as has been said, no real possibility of absolute perfection [in writing a mystery story]. Why? For two main reasons, of which has been stated above in Addenda Note 1. The second is the attitude of the reader himself. Readers are of too many kinds and too many levels of culture. The puzzle addict, for instance, regards the story as a contest of wits between himself and the writer; if he guesses the solution, he has won, even though he could not document his guess or justify it by solid reasoning. There is something of this competitive spirit in all readers, but the reader in whom it predominates sees no value beyond the game of guessing the solution. There is the reader, again, whose whole interest is in sensation, sadism, cruelty, blood, and the element of death. Again there is some in all of us, but the reader in whom it predominates will care nothing for the so-called deductive story, however meticulous. A third class of reader is the worrier-about-the-characters; this reader doesn't care so much about the solution; what really gets her upset is the chance that the silly little heroine will get her neck twisted on the spiral staircase. Fourth, and most important, there is the intellectual literate reader who reads mysteries because they are almost the only kind of fiction that does not get too big for its boots. This reader savors style, characterization, plot twists, all the virtuosities of the writing much more than he bothers about the solution. You cannot satisfy all these readers completely. To do so involves contradictory

elements. I, in the role of reader, almost never try to guess the solution to a mystery. I simply don't regard the contest between the writer and myself as important. To be frank I regard it as the amusement of an inferior type of mind.

13. As has been suggested above, all fiction depends on some form of suspense. But the study of the mechanics of that extreme type called menace reveals the curious psychological duality of the mind of a reader or audience which makes it possible on the one hand to be terrified about what is hiding behind the door and at the same time to know that the heroine or leading lady is not going to be murdered once she is established as the heroine or leading lady. If the character played by Claudette Colbert is in awful danger, we also know absolutely that Miss Colbert is not going to be hurt for the simple reason that she is Miss Colbert. How does the audience's mind get upset by menace in view of this clear knowledge? Of the many possible reasons I suggest two. The intelligence and the emotions function on different levels. The emotional reaction to visual images and sounds, or their evocation in descriptive writing, is independent of reasonableness. The primitive element of fear is never far from the surface of our thoughts; anything that calls to it can defeat reason for the time being. Hence menace makes its appeal to a very ancient and very irrational emotion. Few men are beyond its influence. The other reason I suggest is that in any intense kind of literary or other projection the part is greater than the whole. The scene before the eyes dominates the thought of the audience; the normal individual makes no attempt to reconcile it with the pattern of the story. He is swayed by what is in the actual scene. When you have finished the book, it may, not necessarily will, fall into focus as a whole and be remembered by its merit so considered; but for the time of reading, the chapter is the dominating factor. The vision of the emotional imagination is very short but also very intense.

Revised April 18, 1948

S T O R Y   I D E A :   R E V E N G E

A man, greatly wronged, hunts down another man (who does not know him), makes friends with him, gets his confidence, then starts dropping idle hints which get the hunted man suspicious (without his knowing how to show it). Finally he gets desperate, things begin to happen, and the story ends in an attempt to murder the hero which backfires, killing the hunted man. With a faint enigmatic smile the hero walks out of the story. (He fixed it to backfire—see "The Murder of My Aunt.")

Ideally this should start with the murder of the hero's wife by an unknown, hero suspected—badly roughed around by cops, finally released with much untold on both sides.

(Part used in *The Blue Dahlia*)

In shaving, the side opposite the shaving hand will usually be cut higher on the sideburn than the side on the shaving hand. Use to tell whether a corpse was left-handed.

MARY ROBERTS RINEHART ON THE CRIME NOVEL

from the Saturday Evening Post, *March 11, 1939*

I have written fifteen books about crime. Not thrillers, which bear no relation to life or plausibility, but stories of murder, committed with normal weapons by people otherwise normal. And I am frank to say that I have had a lot of trouble doing it.

The plain fact is that a properly written and developed crime book is really a novel, plus an intricate and partially hidden plot. The writer, in doing one, has pretty nearly as hard a time as the criminal himself. For not only must the characters be real, the setting reasonable and the crime logical. The intricacy of the plot makes it necessary to hold a dozen or a hundred threads in the mind. In doing one I take notes as I go along, but alterations often make these useless; and also I frequently mislay them.

The result is that, in writing such a story, I do the first draft in a sort of frenzy, for fear I may forget something. My pulse goes up, and I have even been known to run a temperature! I do not know how this sort of work affects the others who do it, but the results with me are pretty devastating. The smallest change, too, in the rewriting may necessitate changes all through the book; and if anyone thinks that either easy or funny, one day in my study would show him a haggard wild-eyed woman despairingly searching through mounds of yellow paper for the caliber of a bullet, or tracing the clue of a lost button through four hundred pages of manuscript.

Yet, in its essence, the crime story is simple. It consists of two stories. One is known only to the criminal and to the author himself. It is usually simple, consisting chiefly of the commission of a murder and the criminal's attempt to cover up after it; although quite often he is driven to other murders to protect himself, thus carrying on the suspense.

The other story is the story which is told. It is capable of great elaboration and should, when finished, be complete in itself. It is necessary, however, to connect the two stories throughout the book. This is done by allowing a bit, here and there, of the hidden story to appear. It may be a clue, it may be another crime. In any case, you may be certain that the author is having a pretty difficult time, and that if in the end he fails to explain one of these appearances, at least five hundred people will discover it and write him indignant letters.

Compared with this sort of writing, even the most ponderous tome looks simple.

In fact, it is really the ponderous books which I envy. How easy merely to put down everything you think or imagine. No holding back, no telling oneself that this does not belong, or that. No hewing to the line. No cutting. No fear of letting the interest die. No wastebasket. How wonderful. And how dull!◈

BONDED GOODS

Diamonds Are Forever. *By Ian Fleming (Cape).*
Reviewed by Raymond Chandler

The Sunday Times (*London*), *March 25, 1956*

Some three years ago Mr. Ian Fleming produced a thriller which was about as tough an item as ever came out of England in the way of thriller writing, on any respectable literary level. *Casino Royale* contained a superb gambling scene, a torture scene which still haunts me, and, of couse, a beautiful girl. His second, *Live and Let Die*, was memorable in that he entered the American scene with perfect poise, did a brutal sketch of Harlem and another of St. Petersburg, Florida. His third, *Moonraker*, was, by comparison with the first two explosions, merely a spasm. We now have his fourth book, *Diamonds Are Forever*, which has the preliminary distinction of a sweet title, and of being about the nicest piece of book-making in this type of literature which I have seen for a long time.

Diamonds Are Forever concerns, nominally, the smashing of an international diamond smuggling ring. But actually, apart from the charms and faults I am going to mention, it is just another American gangster story, and not a very original one at that. In Chapter I Mr. Fleming very nearly becomes atmospheric, and with Mr. James Bond as your protagonist, a character about as atmospheric as a dinosaur, it just doesn't pay off. In Chapter II we learn quite a few facts about diamonds, and we then get a fairly detailed description of Saratoga and its sins, and a gang execution which is as nasty as any I have read.

Later there is a more detailed, more fantastic, more appalling description of Las Vegas and its daily life. To a Californian, Las Vegas is a cliché. You don't make it fantastic, because it was designed that way, and it is funny rather than terrifying. From then on there is some very fast and dangerous action, and of course Mr. Bond finally has his way with the beautiful girl. Sadly enough his beautiful girls have no future, because it is the curse of the "series character" that he always has to go back to where he began.

Mr. Fleming writes a journalistic style, neat, clean, spare, and never pretentious. He writes of brutal things, and as though he liked them. The trouble with brutality in writing is that it has to grow out of something. The best hard-boiled writers never try to be tough, they allow toughness to happen when it seems inevitable for its time, place, and conditions.

I don't think *Diamonds Are Forever* measures up to either *Casino Royale* or *Live and Let Die*. Frankly, I think there is a certain amount of padding in it, and there are pages in which James Bond thinks. I don't like James Bond thinking. His thoughts are superfluous. I like him when he is in the dangerous card game; I like him when he is exposing himself unarmed to half a dozen thin-lipped professional killers, and neatly dumping them into a heap of fractured bones; I like him when he finally takes the beautiful girl in his arms and teaches her about one-tenth of the facts of life she knew already.

I have left the remarkable thing about this book to the last. And that is that it is written by an Englishman. The scene is almost entirely American, and it rings true to an American. I am unaware of any other writer who has accomplished this. But let me plead with Mr. Fleming not to allow himself to become a stunt writer, or he will end up no better than the rest of us.

Song At Parting
————————

He left her lying in thenude
    That sultry night in May.
The neighbors thought it rather rude;
    He liked her best that way.

He left a rose beside her head,
    A meat ax in her brain.
A note upon the bureau read:
    "I won't be back again."

                        rc

1941(?)

THE TRAGEDY OF
KING RICHARD III

[Chandler wished to use *The Second Murderer* as a title for his second novel. Blanche Knopf objected and so he countered with *Zounds, He Dies*, which pleased her no better. Eventually, *Farewell, My Lovely* was chosen. The source of his original choice is indicated below.]

SECOND MURDERER: What, shall we stab him as he sleeps?
FIRST MURDERER: No; then he will say 'twas done cowardly when he wakes.

◈   ◈   ◈

FIRST MURDERER: How dost thou feel thyself now?
SECOND MURDERER: Faith, some certain dregs of conscience are yet within me.
FIRST MURDERER: Remember our reward, when the deed is done.
SECOND MURDERER: 'Zounds, he dies: I had forgot the reward.

Act I, Scene 4

She threw her arms around my neck, and nicked my ear with the gunsight.

Take your ears out of the way and I'll leave.

I left her with her virtue intact, but it was quite a struggle. She nearly won.

The only difference between you and a monkey is you wear a larger hat.

All the simple old-fashioned charm of a cop beating up a drunk.

Kropp's Piano Concerto for Two Lame Thumbs

If you don't leave, I'll get somebody who will.

She made a couple of drinks in a couple of glasses you could almost have stood umbrellas in.

Above the sky-blue gabardine slacks he wore a two-tone leisure jacket which would have been revolting on a zebra.

Nothing answered me, not even a stand-in for an echo.

I'm looking for a Mr. Quest. Q as in Quintessential, U as in Uninhibited, E as in Extrasensory, S as in Subliminal, T as in Toots. Put them all together and they spell Brother.

He wanted to buy some sweetness and light and not the kind that comes through the east window of a church.

She sat in front of her princess dresser trying to paint the suitcases out from under her eyes.

I had been stalking the bluebottle fly for five minutes, waiting for him to sit down. He didn't want to sit down. He just wanted to do wing-overs and sing the prologue to *Pagliacci*.

The boys who talk and spit without ever bothering the cigarettes that live in their faces.

Goodnight, goodby and I'd hate to be you.

A ROUTINE TO
SHOCK THE NEIGHBOURS:
FASTER, SLOWER,
NEITHER.

"Well, really, much as one hates to interrupt at a time like this, isn't the tempo—well, one might possibly say a bit adagio?"

"I'm most frightfully sorry. I didn't know you had to catch a train. Do you rather want it presto agitato?"

"Darling, it's not that at all. Well—how does one usually express it?"

"Usually one doesn't. My mistake, of course. Terribly sorry again. I had the notion that as it was such a beastly rainy afternoon, one might possibly spend a few quiet hours—"

"Darling, I simply adore that too. But do they have to be as quiet as this?"

"By quiet, I suppose you mean slow."

"Darling, isn't that slightly a crude word at this time? I meant only that one could spend the hours delightfully—but would they have to be devoted to one performance? Theatres have matinees, occasionally, I'm told."

"I have been so very stupid. Please try to forgive me. (Pause.) Could that be in the slightest degree better, or— or—?"

"Oh, much better darling. I'm afraid—oh, couldn't you please— an occasional pause rather spices the—"

"Conversation, I expect you were about to say. I gather that you mean presto ma non agitato?"

"Exactly, darling, and you are so understanding. And darling, and—oh—oh—darling!"

"Yes, darling?"

"Oh—darling—darling—darling—please don't speak!"

"Not a word."

"Oh, darling, darling, DARLING!—please don't speak."

"I'm not. You're doing all the talking."

"Oh—darling—oh— Oh—oh darling." (Short pause.) Thank you so much, darling—so very, very much. But please—"

"Not a word. Remember?"

"But I like to talk now. Mayn't I?"

"Frankly, darling, you never stopped."

"But this is so different, so quiet, so relaxed, so divinely calm."

"I believe it is still raining."

"I love that. One can waste an entire afternoon with a clear conscience."

"You know, I may sound a bit caddish, but what do you regard as waste? And what do you mean by conscience?"

"Darling, your hand, would you please—"

"Oh dear, I'm really sorry. I must have forgotten."

"Darling, I do have a conscience, you know—at times—mostly between the acts, so to speak."

"It does rather creep in then, doesn't it? After all—"

"All, darling?"

"All so far, anyhow. Do you suppose your conscience could tolerate a small drink at this time?"

"It jolly well better, darling."

(A rather extended pause.)

"Are you comfortable, darling?"

"Heavenly."

"Tempo?"

"Slightly more adagio this time, if you don't really object."

"Object? In this situation? Well, I'm not quite that tempestuous."

"No, of course not darling. I didn't mean that, but—oh—oh—darling—I think I may have misled you—oh darling, darling—"

"Oh. I see. One can't forsee everything, can one?"

"Oh—darling—oh—oh—oh darling—oh—oh—" (Slight pause.)

"You forgot to thank me."

"Well, really. It didn't seem to me all that one-sided. But I do thank you, darling, I do. I'm sorry if—"

"You know I was only teasing you."

"Of course, darling, of course. Forgive me for even mentioning it. What peace! What heavenly peace! I could recite poems—if only I could remember any."

"Not very long ago you said not to speak."

"Darling, I didn't know what I was saying. One rather doesn't. May I remember something now?"

"Not if it is something that happened when you were five years old, please."

"Not that at all. I am remembering being in the back seat of a limousine."

"May I ask with whom?"

"You're a silly man. The driver was in the front seat, if that consoles you at all."

"If he stayed in the front seat."

"I am not sure I like that implication."

"Neither do I. A bit caddish, rather. I do apologize most humbly."

"Darling, your hand."

"My hand? I'm not using it at the moment."

"But darling, I do love it so."

"Oh, oh, of course, darling. Sorry I misunderstood. About the driver?"

"It's so warm, so gentle, so clever."

"You were remembering something, weren't you?"

"Oh yes, darling. But it is so warm— No, what I remembered was that on the back of the driver's seat there was some kind of gadget —I haven't the slimmest as to what it was—but the words were very clear. FASTER SLOWER NEITHER. I was completely without a clue as to what they meant."

"You should have asked the driver. They mean, Presto, Adagio, Intermission."

"I adore you when you speak like that. So witty. Is it intermission now?"

(A pause, not very long.)

"Darling?"

"Yes darling?"

"Please don't speak. Please don't—oh, darling. What I meant was—oh, darling—oh—oh—oh—darling— What I—oh—oh—oh—darling, darling—oh—oh darling one!"

(Author's Note: Over and out. And God help all men on rainy afternoons.)

FINIS

RAILROAD SLANG

J. C. *Furnas*, Saturday Evening Post, *August 21, 1937*

Hog—engine	Brownie—demerit mark
Pike—railroad line	Hotshot—fast train
Reefer—refrigerator car	Drag—slow train freight

Crummy—caboose

SLANG AND HARD TALK

Chicago lightning—gunfire	circulation drops—drinks
dip the bill—take a drink	lip—lawyer
grape—liquor	squibbed off—shot
cough yourself off—beat it	new sweet—new girl
eel juice—liquor	give her hello—say hello to her
creased, bent—knocked off, also stolen	kick the joint—break in

under glass—in prison, caught

HOLLYWOOD SLANG

baggage-smasher—clumsy person

blinker—camera

duchess—a girl in the money

fluff—baby doll

footfever—hurry

garbo—a highhat

jail break—time out to eat

mob it—break formation

queen bee—show off

sock the clock—punch the time clock

toots—chorus boy (getting stale)

X ray—still photo

zubber—a cane and spats guy

NARCOTIC SQUAD SLANG

pin-jabber—hypo user

sniffer—snuffer

dodo—any addict

gow—a dope, as "gowed up"

kick the gong around—use dope (Harlem)

daisy crushers—shoes

pearl diver—dish washer

fancy pants—(verb) to act cagily or coyly

Hard Harry—a hard guy

NOW 15¢

JUNE, 1936

SMASHING **DETECTIVE** STORIES

BLACK MASK

JUNE, 1936

GOLDFISH
By
RAYMOND
CHANDLER

John Drew

BLACK MASK

15 CENTS

KENNEDY and MacBRIDE—Frederick Nebel
FLASHGUN CASEY—George Harmon Coxe
JERRY TRACY—Theodore A. Tinsley

55

NOTE ON THE TOMMY GUN

Quoted by Joseph Gollimb in Crimes of the Year, *Liveright, 1931*

From the catalogue of Peter von Frantzius, Chicago firearms salesman, known as the "armorer to the gangs."

The Thompson gun is an automatic carbine, a new type of firearm combining the portability of a rifle with the effectiveness of a machine gun. It is a .45-calibre gun, weighs nine pounds, eleven ounces, is thirty-three inches long. It is equipped with fine sights, a wind gauge and has a magazine capacity of 100 shots. A compensator, attached to the muzzle, reduces recoil to practically nothing and controls any tendency of the gun to shoot high. One hundred slugs can be aimed and fired in exactly one minute.

To me Marlowe is the American mind; a heavy portion of rugged realism, a dash of good hard vulgarity, a strong overtone of strident wit, an equally strong undertone of pure sentimentalism, an ocean of slang, and an utterly unexpected range of sensitivity. (Used in description of Marlowe sent to Joseph Shaw, editor of Black Mask.)

SAN QUENTIN PRISON SLANG

Quoted by former Warden Holohan in Los Angeles Times

(Well-known terms omitted)

Beak	Judge
Buried	Held incommunicado
Broom	Disappear hastily
Bonarue (Fr.)	Good
Box	Safe and also phonograph
Bank	Shot of dope
Back door parole	Die in prison
Blow your copper	Lose good conduct credits
Buck	Priest
Case dough	Limited money
Caught in a snowstorm	Cocained up
Crazy alley	Fenced-in section for daffy prisoners
Copper-hearted	Informer by nature
Crib	Safe
Crow McGee	No good, not real
Cecil	Cocaine
Croaker	Doctor
Copper	Good prison records
Cop a heel	Assault from behind
Dinah	Nitroglycerine
Dropper	Paid killer
Duffer	Bread

Eye	Detective
Fog	Shoot
Fall money	Bail and legal fees
Fin	Five dollar bill
Fin up	Five years to live
Grease	Protection money
Glom	Steal, grab
Gum heel	Cop
Herder	Guard in prison
Hincty	Suspicious
Jinny	Blind pig
Lifeboat	Pardon, commutation of sentence
McCoy	Genuine (opposed to Crow McGee)
Nose	Police spy
On the Erie	Shut up! Someone is listening.
Office	Signal
On the muscle	Quarrelsome, ready for trouble
Put the cross on	Mark for death
Roscoe	Gat, hand gun
Shag	Worthless
Slam off	Die (not kill)
Swamp	Arrest
Slim	Police spy
Sneeze	Kidnap
Spear	Arrest
Shin	Knife, contraband weapon, shotgun
Siberia	Solitary confinement cells
Tommy Gee	Machine gunner

CRAPS

From May 1936 Easy Money

Possible Points

Number of Point	Ways of throwing it	Chances of throwing
2	1–1	1
3	1–2, 2–1	2
4	1–3, 3–1, 2–2	3
5	1–4, 4–1, 3–2, 2–3	4
6	1–5, 5–1, 2–4, 4–2, 2–3	5
7	1–6, 6–1, 2–5, 5–2, 3–4, 4–3	6
8	2–6, 6–2, 3–5, 5–3, 4–4	5
9	3–6, 6–3, 4–5, 5–4	4
10	4–6, 6–4, 5–5	3
11	5–6, 6–5	2
12	6–6	1
	Possible throws	36

Slang Names of Points

2	Snake-eyes
3	Ace-deuce (not slang)
4	Little Josie
5	Five in the South
6	Jimmy Hix
7	Just seven
8	Ada from Decatur
9	Nina with her hair down
10	Big Dick from Boston
11	None
12	Box car

Crap Rules

Seven or eleven on first throw wins.
Two, three, twelve on first throw loses.
All others are points.
Throws are made until the point makes or seven shows, which latter
  loses.

Betting Odds and True Odds

The bank is eleven to ten to ten.
Play always to the best not considering bets in points.
Anybody can figure this out, if he knows enough mathematics.
On 4 you get three to two—you won't make it, you should get two
  to one.
On 5 and 9 you get three to two, which is just about right.
On 6 and 8 you get even money but you are licked. You should get
  six to five.
Ten same as four.
2, 3, 7, 11, 12 of course cannot be points as they decide the throw in
  the first round, or the round in the first throw, to be more accurate.

Notes in General

To match dice to see if they are honest as to spots, place two
surfaces together whose spots add to seven. Then holding together re-
volve one dice until two apaired surfaces add to seven. Then all paired
and the sum of two end surfaces should add to seven. Otherwise dice are
crooked. Of course that's only one of many ways dice can be crooked.
For instance certain surfaces may be slicker and others rougher. The

slick ones tend to slide and not roll when the first impetus weakens, thus leaving desired faces up. Corners and edges are also doctored to assist or hinder rolling. All the sharper needs is a slight increase on natural percentages. On coin flipping edges are milled to make one side diameter less than the other. A very slight difference will make a percentage in favor of the larger and heavier side falling underneath.

PICKPOCKET LINGO
(MAYBE NEW YORK ONLY)

Saturday Evening Post, *October 21, 1950*

Cannon	General term for pickpocket (Dip is unused, obsolete)
Live cannon	A thief who works on normally situated people, as opposed to a roller (a lushworker) who frisks drunks. Both men knock their victims out. Rousters walk with the victim pretending to help; sneak workers don't touch him unless he is passed out or near to it.
Pit worker	Inside-breast-pocket expert
Moll buzzer	Operator on women's handbags
Sneeze	Arrest
Short	Bus, street car, any public conveyance
Stride	Walking ("On the stride")
Shed	Railroad station
Tip	Crowd
Bridge	Pocket
Button	Police badge
Kiss the dog	Work face to face with the victim
Tail pits	Right and left side pockets of jacket
Pratt	Rear trouser pocket
Stall	Accomplice who creates confusion to fix the victim's attention
Right fall	Grand larceny conviction. To obtain there must be testimony that the accused had his hand in victim's pocket and was caught with the goods still on him. Most arrests are for "jostling," which is a misdemeanor good for no more than six bits (months). A shove is enough when the shover is a known operator.
Hanger binging	Opening women's handbags without stealing the bag.
Tweezer	Change purse
Stiff	A newspaper or other shield to hide operations
Wire or Hook	The actual live cannon, as opposed to the stall
Shot	A young pickpocket just starting to work (Harlem cant)

| Fan the scratch | To locate money in a pocket without putting the hand in, i.e., by touch |
| Dunnigan worker | Thieves who hang around comfort stations hoping for a coat left on a hook |

Note: A cannon never *takes* your money. He forks his fingers over it and moves you away from it with a shove.

NOTE ON TYPEWRITER RIBBON CODE DATING

The number on the back of the box, e.g. F6322V, is the date written backwards. The letter V expresses the month, determined by eliminating all the letters of the alphabet before K. V is thus the 12th or December. The rest of the number in reversed order, i.e. 2236 is the day of the month and the year. The date on this ribbon is thus December 22 1936. The letter F at the beginning of the reversed number is probably the type ribbon color and degree of inking, or maybe just color and degree of inking, as each type also has a name, e.g. Remtico. But this last is just guesswork. As to the letter which starts the year, it can of course be varied, and probably is, i.e. K is January in this set-up, but January could be any letter.

SIMILES AND COMPARISONS

As noiseless as a finger in a glove

Lower than a badger's balls (!!) (Vulgar—belly)

As systematic as a madam counting the take

About as French as a doughnut (i.e. not French at all)

His face was long enough to wrap twice around his neck

As much sex appeal as a turtle

A nose like a straphanger's elbow

As clean as an angel's neck

Smart as a hole through nothing

A face like a collapsed lung

So tight his head squeaks when he takes his hat off

As cold as a nun's breeches

High enough to have snow on him

As shiny as a clubwoman's nose

He sipped like a hummingbird drinking dew from a curled leaf

As gaudy as a chiropractor's chart

A mouth like wilted lettuce

His smile was wide, about three quarters of an inch

A thready smile

As cold as Finnegan's feet

As rare as a fat postman (Cissy)

The triangular eye of a squirrel

Longer than a round trip to Siam

As cute as a washtub

Lonely as a caboose of a fifty car freight

A great long gallows of a man with a ravaged face and a haggard eye

A sea sick albatross

Similes - including comparisons

As rare as a ... feature (...) ...

As loud as a fork bend

As dull as a football interview   L.S

As clean as ... Harrett's guest room (...?)

As systematic as a ... country ... ...

So big as a dirty joke in a sentry ...

As gaudy as a chiropractor's shirt   L.S

Lower than a dachy's ... (!!) vulgar ... L.S

No more charm than a mantel (...?)   L.S

Lonely as ... for July or ...

No more personality than a paper cup   ...?) L.S

... harder as a doughnut (... not ... ...)

His face was long enough ... ...   L.S

As genial as a ... ...

So graceful as a Chopin ...   L.S

Like the little dog that ran around and ... after the big dog.

To ... to light a Scotchman's ...

Longer than a second trip to ...   L.S

... your ... ... - To ...

As soothing as a piano ...   L.S

As explosive as a nail keg   L.S

As lonely as a ... lover   L.S

As much sex appeal as a ...   L.S

As ... ... the eyes of a ... dog.   L.S

A ... like a ...   L.S

THE HOLLYWOOD BOWL

[Excerpted from a review of *The Golden Egg* by James S. Pollak, which appeared in *The Atlantic Monthly*, January 1947.]

My real interest is in the Hollywood novel as a type. It interests me because it has never been licked and I want to suggest my own idea of why it has never been licked. It is invariably about the wrong things. The novel (I don't care how long it is) deals with persons in confined spaces, just as does the play. These persons, the characters, are over-simplified for emphasis and oversharpened for effect. That is to say, they are played in an artificial perspective. But the instant you make a huge and complicated industry the background of such an affair, your perspective is lost. You cannot write a novel about United States Steel and at the same time deal with the weekend binge of a third vice-president. You cannot make a close-up and a long shot in the same "take." There is no lens that will photograph it. And you cannot show the inner workings, the superb skills, the incredible idiocies, the glory, the opulence, the grandeur and the decay, the poignant humanity and the icy heart-lessness of this magnificent yet childish colossus, the movie business, in the terms of a hot-pants actress, an egomaniac director, a snide execu-tive, four frantic secretaries, and a sweet young thing in an open Cadil-lac.

You can only write about the waste, and the waste is not the story. *The Last Tycoon*, by far the best of them all, most clearly (per-haps for that very reason) reveals this futility. Monroe Stahr, its hero, is magnificent when he sticks to the business of dealing with pictures and the people he has to use to make them; the instant his personal life as a love-hungry and exhausted man enters the picture, he becomes just another guy with too much money and nowhere to go. Perhaps, had Scott Fitzgerald lived, he might have written the story and thrown out the nonsense. I do not think so, but the hope lies with his dust.

The story that is Hollywood will some day be written and it will not primarily be about people at all, but about a process, a very living and terrible and lovely process, the making of a single picture, almost any hard-fought and ambitious picture, but preferably a heart-breaker to almost everyone concerned. In that process will be all the agony and heroism of human affairs, and it will be all in focus, because the process will be the story. Everything that matters in Hollywood goes into this process. The rest is waste. Above all the vice is waste, and the vicious people, of whom there are many and always will be, because Hollywood is starved for talent, for a single facet of a single talent, and will pay the price in disgust, because it has to. Why should it not? The theater always has, and the theater is a pygmy compared with Hollywood.

SOME RARE COOKED VIANDS FROM A BEVERLY HILLS SPECIALTY SHOP CATERING TO MOVIE PEOPLE

Culled from Philip K. Scheuer, Los Angeles Times, *October 4, 1936*

Sugarless jam and jellies and vintage marmalade from Oxford; honeys from Greece, Smyrna, Portugal, Syria and the Ionian Islands; turtle soup from the Caribbean and marrons glacés from France; escargots, neatly tinned from the same country; goose liver in port wine from Strasbourg; Bar-le-duc currant jelly; "Bombay Duck" (really Bummalow fish from India); roast partridges and pigeons in sour cream from Holland; Dutch sausages; toheroas, a kind of giant clam, from New Zealand; white bait from the same place; Norwegian trout in jelly; caviar kept at 28 degrees ever since it was torn from the mother sturgeon in Russia; bird's nest and shark's fin soups from China; also fried rice birds in tins from China; poppadums from India, made of meal, that, when dropped into hot butter, curl into fancy shapes; from Turkey preserves of bergamot blossoms and rose petals; yerba mate from South America with a gourd and bombilla to sip it through; California ripe olives as large as plums; cockscombs and kidneys, financiere, from France.

A QUALIFIED FAREWELL

About a year and a half ago, when several motion picture producers were tripping over their secretaries in their rush to sign me up for some inexpensive project, it happened that the last producer I had actually worked for spent about fifteen minutes of time and three or four inches of a personalized cigar telling my agent that, vastly to his surprise, I was not a sole screenplay writer at all. There was a time when I would have crept into the darkest corner of the clothes closet and buried my face in my mother's Sunday dress and cried my little heart out over a thing like this. But I don't know, I don't seem to care any more. I seem to have reached that stage of intellectual degradation where the warm blood courses through me gaily when I am praised and my mind kind of goes blank when I am dispraised. Anyhow, the fellow was quite right. I am not a sole screenplay writer, if by this crack is meant a creative artist who can all by himself produce a clean and wholesome shooting script which, as it stands, will satisfy all concerned and fill them with jubilation. I am just not that good. At the risk of being thought a cad, may I ask who is? A few writer-directors may occur to you who seem to get their stuff on celluloid without much recorded interference, and maybe a few writer-producers. I even know of one head of an organization who, when too jaded for more important activities, will bat out a complete screenplay all by himself—or that's what the frame says—and is considered to be a terrific writer, except possibly by the people who do not work for him. There may even be two or three practitioners who just write, and somebody really comes along and shoots the stuff as is. I am not in their class. After approximately five years of working for Hollywood, I know that I wasn't meant to be. And the only purpose of this brittle little communication is to suggest to you, dear reader, that I don't want to be, and why.

I am not trying to knock the art or profession of writing for the screen. This has to do with my private conception of what writing is, and what a writer is entitled to get out of his work, other than money. It has to do with magic and emotion and vision, with the free flow of images, thoughts, and ideas, with discipline that comes from within and is not imposed from without. It has to do with that sense of power over one's medium which comes not frequently and lasts not long, and is one of the least egotistical emotions in the world, because one knows perfectly well it is merely an established communication with the subconscious mind. It has to do with that rare facility of expression which has nothing to do with conscious technique, since technique bears the same relation to it as a grammarian bears to a poet. Without this or the hope of it, writing is a lost endeavor. Without magic, there is no art. Without art, there is no idealism. Without idealism, there is no integrity. Without integrity, there is nothing but production, and in the end not even that, since showmanship on the most frankly commercial level contains an element of incessant striving for perfection, if it be only a perfection of detail.

The case-hardened veterans of the picture business will probably consider my remarks a little too high-flown for practical politics. Perhaps they are. As a critic of the processes of film making, I have grave faults, the most glaring of which is that I don't know enough about the business. If I did, I should either have lost the impulse to criticize or I should have been long since committed to a way of life which made it dangerous for me to criticize in any effective manner. The dilemma of the critic has always been that if he knows enough to speak with authority, he knows too much to speak with detachment. A little less than three years ago, when I knew a lot less than I know now, I wrote a rather petulant article about the position of the writer in Hollywood. I was told it gave great umbrage to the executives of the studio where I was then under contract, and that it had done me a lot of harm with the producers. I never had any tangible evidence of this, but I am willing to assume that it was so. It was at a time when the box-office take was automatically terrific, when the only way you could make an unprofitable picture was not to make it. In the glow of such success any criticism of the methods which produced it may have appeared impertinent. If the boys in the front office still feel that way, and I am not sure that they do, this is a kind of impertinence they are going to have to get used to. Hollywood's failure to find an enlightened way of dealing with creative people is no longer merely a matter of bruised egos. It is a failure of a method of making pictures, and the results of this failure are showing up at the box office. You can't make good pictures without good screenplays, and you can't get good screenplays from people who do not know how to write them, technically speaking; or who do know how to write them, technically speaking, but have been debauched and spoiled by Hollywood to such an extent that technique is all they have left. Technique alone is never enough. You have to have passion. Technique alone is just an embroidered pot holder.

To write effectively for the screen you have to understand the grim obstacles and the mechanical processes which intervene between the script and the final negative. Within the padded horsehair frame of a mid-Victorian censorship, you are supposed to create an illusion of objective truth which it is one of the main purposes of that censorship to suppress. You go in with dreams, and you come out with the Parent-

Teachers Association. A number of the commonest and most forcible words in the English language, no more fundamentally obscene than a candlestick, are taboo because somewhere, somehow, somebody connected them with an impure or irreligious thought. There is probably no facet of American life which you can accurately portray, but you can photograph Clark Gable in his underpants, you can dissolve out on an adulterous kiss, and you can be more obscene by implication than the forthright smut talk of soldiers in a barrack room. The terminal result of this straightjacket Grundyism is intellectual lethargy and paralysis of the imagination. What's the use of thinking up strong dramatic stories or scenes when you know in advance they are going to turn out as tame as Prudence Penny's recipe for baked custard?

The next hazard is the producer, or rather the function of a producer. My friend Joe Sistrom privately and in print has defined this function as well as it can be defined by a man who is far too intelligent to be considered a typical producer, a man who, without any pretensions whatsoever to being a writer, contributed several of its most brilliant lines to one of the most brilliant motion picture scripts ever written. I refer, without embarrassment, to *Double Indemnity*. And yet in a sense the more intelligent and forceful a producer is, the more numbing his effect on the creative thinking of a writer. The weak producer makes you solve your own problems and write your own story. The strong producer takes it away from you and makes it his story. Granted that he is the writer's best friend. Often he is his only friend. Gently, deftly, and with almost infinite patience he will create about the writer that rosy illusion that he is working in an artistic medium, and that even the scenes that regretfully had to be thrown away were graven on the producer's heart, and in the lonely watches of the night he tells them over to himself and weeps. He will charm the writer in his despair, soothe him in his arrogance, and when the artistic temperament goes haywire the producer will take him by the hand and slowly, methodically, and thoroughly get him paralyzed drunk. Perhaps the producer can't think of a decent line to save his life, but he will worry himself to a frazzle making you think of one. With how delicate a touch will he remove the subtleties from your story, because he knows damn well the yahoos in the balcony can't tell a subtlety from a goldfish. With how fatherly a tenderness will he etherize your imagination, because he knows imagination is poison at the box office. How sadly will he drain the life blood from your story and hand you back the embalmed remains as if it was just what you wanted—or at least what you ought to want, if you are a reasonable fellow and willing to face the facts of life. It is not what you started out to write, nor as a rule is it even what the producer hoped you would write. But, all in all, it is probably a respectable and adequate script. It is the right length, more or less; the scenes play fairly well, more or less, if the director will let them and if the stars think they have enough lines; the dialogue probably sounds quite businesslike; and only a much closer scrutiny than it can get at the current speed of projection will disclose its essential emptiness and triviality. It may not be quite the dashing hunk of drama or comedy you set out to fabricate, but after all it's just another Hollywood picture. In a couple of years it will be as dead as Julius Caesar and a damn sight deader than Cleopatra.

What did you expect to get out of screenwriting anyway—a pride of achievement, a sense of mastery over a difficult and exacting medium, and perhaps along the way a little pure joy? All this and money, too? Rather ridiculous, isn't it? Permit me to be ridiculous with you. I, too, make these impossible demands, well knowing that they are impossible and that the reason is basic to the mechanics of picture making. The content of a motion picture is character and emotion and situation, and the combination of these things into drama. This is the result of an act of pure creation. At one moment there is nothing, at another there are words on paper: dialogue and stage directions cast in a certain form which is called a screenplay. And yet even on paper this has no real existence. It has to be photographed on celluloid. The writing of a screenplay is drudgery, partly because it is a difficult form and intrinsically unsatisfying, and partly because ninety-nine people know more about how it should be done than the one who does it. In this respect screenwriting is unique among the literary arts. In all the others the writer may be good or bad, but he is supposed to know what he is doing. But no screenwriter knows what he is doing. It takes somebody who is not a writer to tell him what he is doing. I am not indignant about this situation. I am not even prepared to suggest a remedy. Still less would I suggest that the thousand-odd active members of the Screen Writers Guild are by definition screenwriters, or in fact any kind of writers. Many of them are obviously nothing of the sort. My real concern is that those among them who *are* writers and have proved it in other fields simply can't get any real fun out of screenwriting. All they can get is money, and if money satisfies them, they are not writers. It does not satisfy me. I don't care how much they pay me, unless they can also give me delight in the work. They can't. And if you regard this situation, not from the point of view of a few soreheads or unreasonable people such as I may happen to be, but from the point of view of the broad problem of making pictures, and good ones, out of screenplays, and good ones, it becomes rather obvious that, until screenwriting is a rewarding kind of work in other than a financial sense, the creative standards of the motion picture will grow progressively worse rather than better. Because Hollywood is no longer the only golden vineyard for writers. Even if it were, money, like other commodities, can be priced out of the market. The record shows that Hollywood has rarely been able to buy first-class writing talent or to keep it if bought. It is becoming increasingly obvious that it can hardly buy even the best of the second-raters, since these can make as much money writing books of fiction and selling the motion picture rights as they can by writing directly for the screen. And as for security, again let the record speak. There is no security. There never was.

We have in our midst a group of people who appear to suffer from a quaint anemia of the reasoning faculty, a sort of constitutional weakness such as is observed in royal families that intermarry too much. These seem to believe that, as screenwriters, they should own and control the uses of their writings and should, at the same time, be maintained in reasonable luxury by the people who take all the financial risks. So stated, the thesis is absurd, but it is not as absurd as it looks. The absurdity is not so much in the demand itself as in the definition of those who are entitled to make the demand. Since the processes of picture making as practiced in Hollywood are such that they destroy the independence and artistic courage of screenwriters, then the least the industry can give them in return is some kind of insurance against fear. A great many bad pictures are made in Hollywood because the men and women who wrote them are afraid to hold out against the dictates of gimcrack showmen. Integrity is a nice word, and you hear it a great deal in Hollywood, but you seldom meet the quality itself. The employment of a writer is subject to the whim of producers and executives, contract or no contract. Leaving aside the obvious incompetents on the one hand and the obvious crooks on the other, there are very few screenwriters who can tell important producers to go to hell and get away with it. Yet this is what integrity is—an act of courage and defiance performed at the risk of losing your job, and for no personal gain but the desire to do that job a little better than they want you to do it. Even if you have the courage, you get tired of using it. There is so little at stake in an artistic sense; not an ideal, merely a slightly more dignified compromise between creativeness and commercialism. If you oppose the routine minds, they are angered by your opposition. If you do not oppose them, they say you are a hack without integrity. What Hollywood seems to want is a writer who is ready to commit suicide in every story conference. What it actually gets is the fellow who screams like a stallion in heat and then cuts his throat with a banana. The scream demonstrates the artistic purity of his soul, and he can eat the banana while somebody is answering a telephone call about some other picture.

And just what is it he is fighting for, anyway? He is not going to make the picture. The people who are going to make it, the producer, the director, the cameraman, the actors, and the cutters are far too strong-minded to permit themselves to become script addicts. Allow me to refer you to the words of Mr. Gregg Toland as reported by Lester Koenig in the December number of our parish magazine. One of the questions Mr. Koenig put to Mr. Toland was, "What happens to the camera directions they (the writers) put into their screenplays in capital letters?" Mr. Toland's answer: "Directors and cameramen over the years have developed a method of reading script so they do not see these directions at all. The director can't work out staging and mechanics in his office, so why should the writer worry about trucking shots, etc. Usually he's talking about a subject of which he has a very limited knowledge. Writers like Sherwood write in master scenes and don't go into detailed camera instructions. That's the way it should be." As a slightly meager creative artist in this fascinating medium, I am fascinated by the implication of these words. They are spoken with the authority of one who, not being a writer, inevitably knows far more about screenwriting than I shall ever know. Would it startle Mr. Toland to learn that the screenwriter regards the camera as his principal character, and that if he did not write a part for that character he would not be writing a screenplay? He doesn't write in camera movements for the benefit of the director or the cameraman, but for his own benefit: so that he may have some knowledge of the acting length of the script; so that he may leave out of his dialogue those effects which the camera can better achieve without words; so that he may have some feeling for the rhythm and pace and movement of the film across the screen. The writer knows perfectly well that the director will not follow his camera directions literally. For one thing, he doesn't know who the director is going to be. The styles and methods of directors vary, not only from man to man but from year to year and from picture to picture; if they are imaginative enough, as a few directors are, even from scene to scene. Some directors move their camera constantly, slide in and out of close-ups, pan all over the set. Others use static shots and cut back and forth. Some like dissolves and will use two dissolves to get a character up a flight of stairs. Others hate dissolves and will only use them when they are absolutely forced to. Some directors will follow a long movement in silence because they know how to make the movement exciting in itself. Others can't get a character out of the front door in silence, because their lack of pictorial inventiveness is so great that they must have dialogue to cover the simplest excursion. And speaking of dialogue, Mr. Toland again hits the bull's eye with a handful of potato salad. "My advice to writers," he adds, "would be to concentrate their worrying on the content of the scene and the dialogue." Which dialogue did you mean, Mr. Toland? The stuff that's in the script or what comes off the screen after the director gets through fixing it up? My acquaintance with directors at work is not vast, I admit, but I have only met two who did not consider themselves eminently qualified to improve in a couple of minutes a sequence of dialogue which may have been revised and polished and repolished twenty times before the director ever saw it. And by an odd coincidence, these gentlemen come from European countries where the literary quality of screenwriting is far ahead of ours.

If any of the remarks heretofore set down in this essay should be thought offensive, let me say that I should be the first to congratulate myself. They can be offensive only to those whom it is my pleasure and right and even my duty to offend. My authority does not go beyond the honesty of my belief. I am no superb technician or inexorable scene-squeezer like Billy Wilder. I am the man who produces the raw material on which the superb technique can be exercised, the man who writes the scenes that wait to be squeezed. If I were more, I should also be less, and the more I should be would, from my point of view, not be worth the less I should be. I am not paid large sums of money for writing camera angles, although I do this because I must, even if I do it badly. This is precisely the article of my complaint. In Hollywood you cannot acquire the technical dexterity without at the same time losing the power of creating the thing on which the dexterity feeds. If I cannot have mastery of the medium, I cannot have freedom, and if I cannot have freedom, the money is not enough. There are a hundred technicians for every one man who in five pages of dialogue can make characters come alive and create the emotional tension between them that constitutes drama. Hollywood needs the one man more than it needs the hundred, but it cannot give him joy. It can only give him figures on a check. There is something wrong here which in my opinion does not have to be wrong. The picture makers are not all stupid people, yet they deal with writers as if these were curious half-witted creatures with some inexplicable gift of putting into words the ideas of other men and, under severe supervision, in a form adapted to photography. This is sometimes true. As another friend of mine remarked, Hollywood does a great job with lousy writers; it beats them with bull whips and dazzles them with gold and somehow it gets out a script. With a few modifications, which are little more than polite gestures, Hollywood deals in much the same way with all writers. But you cannot deal that way with good writers. Because the thing which makes them valuable to you cannot be controlled by people who are not writers. Hollywood ought to have found this out by now, but it hasn't, and I think the principal reason why it hasn't is that Hollywood is not really a civilized community. It is provincial, inbred, narrow, and immersed in a complication of techniques which were once enough to dominate the world but are no longer enough to dominate even the United States. Its big men are mostly little men with fancy offices and a lot of money. A great many of them are stupid little men, with reach-me-down brains, small-town arrogance, and a sort of animal knack of smelling out the taste of the stupidest part of the public. They are not in a class with the men who run big railroads, banks, insurance companies, publishing houses, or industrial corporations. They have played in luck so long that they have come to mistake luck for enlightenment. They trade too hard when the going is good, and they scare too easily when it isn't. In a crisis they become hysterical. For statesmanship they substitute intrigue. They know how to deal with agents and temperamental stars, most of whom could drop dead tomorrow with little or no effect on the essential processes of picture making. But the creative use of talent, which is the essential foundation of the motion picture business, the rulers do not understand at all, or they would long since have sought to create the circumstances in which it can flourish. All they can do is pay for it and wait for delivery. If you are a writer and an honest one, you try very hard to make delivery, but too many things get in the way, too many hands maul you, there are too many words in your ears and too much stale thinking that makes you stale yourself, and in the end, however hard you try, all you get is tired.

The five years I have spent in and around the motion picture studios come pretty close to being a Hollywood generation. In that rather brief space of time I have seen a stock girl who could not get a small part become a star on another lot. I have seen a young and competent mystery novelist assigned to write an original screenplay, without any experience of the form or anyone to help him, get fired because the result was naturally somewhat disappointing, and become a successful director with another company in no time at all. I have seen almost the entire personnel (except actors) of a large studio dissolve into thin air and be replaced by a collection of cut-rate amateurs and "B" picture impresarios, and all this with no apparent effect on the earning power of the organization. I have seen world-famous novelists move from studio to studio and assignment to assignment month after month and year after year, without ever once in the entire period achieving a single scene (not to mention a whole script) professional enough to be put before the camera. The old reliable hacks are still around, or if they are not, those who have taken their places look just like them. We still have the constructionists who can't write, the dialogue men who can't plot, the brain pickers who brush off your ideas and then try to sell them back to you next day as their own, and the credit hogs who would rather spoil the best script they ever saw than not get their names on the title sheet.

Perhaps I had better say *you* still have all these things, because I am moving to another climate. Please don't misunderstand me. The motion picture as an art is not in question. I think pictures like *Variety, The Last Laugh, Sous les Toits de Paris, Mayerling, Open City, Odd*

Man Out, Stagecoach, The Informer, and others of their quality make the strained effects of the stage look silly, although at its best the stage has a certain high magic which the motion picture has so far failed to achieve. But such pictures are extremely rare, and even if I had the ability to write one, I have not patience to wait for the precise combination of luck and power and talent that makes one possible. The qualifications for permanent success in Hollywood, which I lack, are a tremendous enthusiasm for the work in hand, coupled with an almost complete indifference to the use which will be made of it. The future of the motion picture is in the hands of that small group of people who will break their necks to achieve something beautiful with the almost certain knowledge that it will be spoiled by vulgarians. If there are enough of them, and if they can last out the ordeal long enough, the day may come when it will not be spoiled. The self-appointed spokesmen for the motion picture industry, much as they differ on other matters, seem to be well agreed that the story is the thing, and that the story is bad, and that the writer is the villain. My friends, let us bow our heads in humble gratitude. For this brief moment in the frozen limelight we stand alone. We are the architects of failure. Star billing at last! Peace—it's wonderful!

With these touching words I bid you farewell. I have enjoyed writing this piece, although essentially I know it is a testament of failure. If it were merely a personal failure, the piece would not be worth writing. I think it is much more. A man does not deliberately turn his back on what I could get out of Hollywood from motives of personal pique or overinflated vanity. Such moods pass. Mine has been with me for a long time. I have a sense of exile from thought, a nostalgia of the quiet room and the balanced mind. I am a writer, and there comes a time when that which I write has to belong to me, has to be written alone and in silence, with no one looking over my shoulder, no one telling me a better way to write it. It doesn't have to be great writing, it doesn't even have to be terribly good. It just has to be mine.

"No art can survive on a purely mechanical inspiration. When the film has exhausted its technical élan, then it must inevitably return to the poets."

—from Herbert Read, Towards Film Aesthetics, *(1932)*

The
Scrapbook

1905

1918

1949

1958

1958

English Summer

A Gothic Romance

by

Raymond Chandler

Illustrated by Edward Gorey

Bury me where the soldiers of retreat
Are buried, underneath the faded star.
                    —Stephen Vincent Benét
                    (*Motto for* English Summer)

1.

It was one of those old, old cottages in the country which are supposed to be picturesque, which the English go to for weekends or for a month in the summer in a year when they can't afford the high Alps or Venice or Sicily or Greece or the Riviera, a year when they don't want to see their infernal gray ocean.

In the winter who lives in such places? Who would slog through the long, dreadful wet silence to find out? But probably some peaceful old woman with apple cheeks and two earthen hot-water bottles in her bed and not a care in the world, not even for death.

It was summer now, however, and the Crandalls were there for a month, I, as a guest for a vague few days. Edward Crandall had invited me himself, and I had gone, a little to be near her, a little because his asking me was a sort of insult, and I like insults, from some people.

I don't think he hoped to catch me making love to her. I don't think he would have cared. He was too busy on the tiles of the roofs, on the walls of the barnyards, in the shadows of the hayricks. He wouldn't have paid either of us that compliment anyhow.

But I never had made love to her, so he couldn't have caught us—not in the three years, off and on, I had known them. It was a curious, a very naïve, a very decrepit delicacy on my part. In the circumstances, while she continued to endure him in utter silence, I thought it would have been too callous a gesture. Perhaps I was wrong. Probably I was wrong. She was very lovely.

It was a small cottage, at the extreme edge of a village called Buddenham, but in spite of its natural seclusion it had those unnecessary walls that some English gardens have, as though the flowers might be caught in embarrassing postures. The part in the back, nearest the house, they liked to call the "close." It had that almost unbearable fragrance of English flowers in summer. On the sunny side nectarines grew in espaliers, and there was a table put there on the firm, ancient lawn, and rustic chairs for tea, if it was warm enough for tea outdoors. It never was while I was there.

In front there was more garden, another walled-in space smelling of roses and mignonettes, drowsy with striped bumblebees. There was a walk and a hedge and a fence and a gate. That was outside. I liked all of that. Inside I hated one thing, the stairs. They had a sort of deadly cold ingenuity of wrongness, as though designed for your six months' bride to fall down and break her neck, and make one of those sudden tragedies that people used to gloat over, licking their tear-wet lips.

I didn't even mind there being only one bathroom and no shower. After ten years of visiting in England, for long periods at a time, I knew there were few houses, even large ones, with more. And you get used to being wakened in the morning by a discreet tapping, then the door opening softly without your having answered, then the curtains being rasped back, and then by the dull thud of a copper utensil of quaint shape, full of hot water, being deposited in a wide shallow tray, in which you can just manage to sit—if you put your wet feet out on the floor. This is old-fashioned now, but it persists in some places.

That was all right, but not the stairs. In the first place there was a sort of very vague half-turn at the top, in complete darkness, and a totally unnecessary half-step there, at exactly the worst possible angle. I always stumbled over it. Then at the straight upper reach of the main flight, before the half-turn, there was a nowel post as hard and sharp as a steel girder and about the size of a well-grown oak. It was carved, the story went, from the rudder stem of some Spanish galleon which a very English storm had cast upon a very English lee shore. After the usual few centuries, part of the rudder-stem had got to Buddenham and got itself made into a nowel post.

One more thing—the two steel engravings. They hung out at an absurd angle from the wall right on the straight part of the stairs—and the stairs were already cramped. They hung side by side, framed in that very monumental manner steel engravings used to love. One corner would lay your skull open like an ax. They were the Stag Drinking and the Stag at Bay. They seemed to be exactly the same, except for the position of the stag's head. But I never really saw them. I just crawled past them. The only place from which you could really see them was the passage to the kitchen and the scullery. From there, if you had any business there, and if you liked steel engravings after Landseer, you could look up through the banisters and gaze your fill. It may have been a lot of fun, but not to me.

This particular afternoon I came down these stairs stumbling and dodging about as usual, swinging my cherrywood stick in a brisk and British manner, getting it caught in the banisters, and inhaling the faint sour aroma of the paste behind the wallpaper.

The house seemed unusually still. I missed the cracked mono-tone of old Bessie's humming in the kitchen. Old Bessie went with the cottage and looked very much as though she had come ashore with the Spanish galleon, through a lot of rocks.

I peeped into the drawing room, and that was empty, so I went on back through the French doors to the "close." Millicent was sitting there, in a garden chair. Just sitting. It seems that I must describe her, and I shall probably overdo it, like the rest.

She was, I suppose, very English, but more fragile than the English. She had that sort of ceramic delicacy and grace, like certain very lovely kinds of china. She was rather tall—quite tall, in fact, and from certain angles may have appeared a trifle sharp. But I had never thought so. And above all she had the flowing movement, the infinite, effortless grace of a fairy tale. She had the pale hair, so pale, so gold, so fine that you never saw a separate strand of it. It was the hair of a princess in a remote and bitter tower. It was the hair an old nurse would have brushed, hour after hour by candlelight, in a vast dim room, holding it softly in tired old hands, while the princess sat before a polished silver mirror, half asleep, and glanced into the burnished metal occasionally, but not to see herself. She had dreams for that mirror. That was the sort of hair Millicent Crandall had. I touched it only once and then it was too late.

She had lovely arms too, and they seemed to know it, without, as it were, her knowing it. So that they always seemed poised in just the right way, in the most languid and gracious curves, along a mantelpiece, with the wrist trailing, or the edge of a rather severe sleeve falling away so straightly that the curve it let you glimpse gained strength and lost no loveliness. And at tea, her hands would make gracious, unheeded, beautiful motions over the silver. That would be in London, particularly in the long, gray upstairs drawing room they had there. It would be half raining, and the light would be the color of rain, and the paintings on the wall, whatever color they had in them, would be gray. Even if they were van Goghs they would be gray. But her hair would not be gray.

Today, however, I just looked at her and waggled the cherry-wood stick and said, "No use asking you to walk over to the lake and let me row you about, I suppose?"

She half smiled. Her half smile was negative.

"Where's Edward? Golfing?"

The same half smile, but derision in it now.

"Something about rabbits today, with a gamekeeper he met in the village pub. It *would* be a gamekeeper. It seems a lot of them get around a sort of clearing in a spinney, a warren, and the ferrets are sent down into the rabbits' holes, and so the rabbits have to come up."

"I know," I said. "Then they drink the blood."

"That should have been my line, if you ever left me one. Run along now, and don't be too late back for tea."

"It must be fun," I said, "just waiting for tea. In a warm spot, in a nice garden, with the bees droning around you not too close, and the nectarines perfuming the air. Waiting for tea—as if it were a revolution."

She just looked at me with her pale blue English eyes. Not tired eyes, but eyes that had looked at the same things too long.

"Revolution? What in the world does that mean?"

"I don't know," I said frankly. "It just sounded like a good gag line. So long."

To the English, Americans are always a trifle stupid.

I walked over to the lake too fast. It wasn't much of a lake, as American lakes go, but it had a lot of tiny islands on it, and these made vistas and gave a false impression of length, and the water birds swooped and clattered or just sat on reeds growing out of the water and looked supercilious. In places the old backwoods strolled down very close to the gray water. In these places there were no water birds. Somebody's cracked but not somehow leaky old tub was tied to a log by a short rope, stiff with age and paint. I used to row that among the little islands. Nothing lived on them, but there were things growing, and now and again some old gaffer would stop hoeing and shade his eyes and stare at me. I would call out a polite semi-English greeting. He would not answer. He was too old, too deaf and had other uses for his energy.

I got more tired than usual that day. The old boat seemed as cumbersome as a water-logged barn in a Mississippi flood. The always too short oars were shorter than ever. So I loafed going back, and there were shafts of yellow light through the beeches, distantly, in another world. It got cold on the water.

I dragged the boat up high enough to tie the painter to the log and straightened, sucking a finger the knot hadn't been kind to.

I hadn't heard a sound of her or of her big black horse or even of the clinking rings at the end of the bit. Last year's leaves must have been very soft around there, or she had a magic with horses.

But when I straightened and turned she was not more than nine feet away.

She wore a black riding habit, a white hunting stock at her throat, and the horse looked wicked as she sat astride of him. A stallion. She smiled, a black-eyed woman, young, but not a girl. I had never seen her before. She was terribly handsome.

"Like rowing?" she inquired in that offhand English way that is utterly beyond mere ease. Her voice was the voice of a thrush, an American thrush.

The black stallion looked at me red-eyed and quietly pawed a leaf or two, then stood like a rock, quietly swinging one ear.

"Hate it," I said. "All hard work and blisters. Then three miles home for tea."

"Then why do you do it? I never do anything I don't like." She touched the stallion's neck with a gauntleted glove as black as his coat.

I shrugged. "I must like it in a way. Exercise. Takes the nerves out of you. Beats up an appetite. I can't think of any clever reasons."

"You should," she said. "Being an American."

"Am I an American?"

"Of course. I watched you rowing. So fierce. I knew even then. And of course, your accent."

My eyes must have been a little avid on her face, but she didn't seem to mind.

"Staying with some people called Crandall, at Buddenham, aren't you, Mr. American? Gossip does get around so in these country places. I'm Lady Lakenham, from Lakeview."

Something must have stiffened in my face. As if I had said out loud: Oh, you're *that* woman!

She noticed it, I dare say. She would notice most things. Perhaps all things. But not even a very small new shadow was born in her deep black, depthless eyes.

"That lovely Tudor place—I've seen it already—from a distance."

"See it closer and get a shock," she said. "Try my tea. The name, if you please?"

"Paringdon. John Paringdon."

"John's a nice sturdy name," she said. "A trifle on the dull side. I'll have to put up with it, during the brief moments of our acquaintance. Take hold of Romeo's stirrup leather, John—above the iron and lightly."

The stallion fretted a little when I touched the leather, but she cooed at him and he began to walk homeward, up a rise, slowly, his ears very alert. Even when some bird suddenly whirred across the glade, low under the trees, only his ears jumped.

"Nice manners," I said.

She arched her black eyebrows.

"Romeo? That depends. We meet all sorts of people, don't we, Romeo? And our manners vary."

She swung her short whip lightly.

"But that wouldn't concern you, would it?"

"I don't know," I said. "It might."

She laughed. I found out later that she very seldom laughed.

My hand on the stirrup leather was inches above her foot. I wanted to touch her foot. I didn't know why; I thought she wanted me to touch her foot. I didn't know the why of that either.

"Oh, you have nice manners too," she said. "I can see that."

I said, "I'm still not sure. They are swift like the swallow, and slow like the ox, but always in the wrong place."

The whip flicked around idly, but not at me, nor at the black stallion who obviously didn't expect it to flick at him.

"I'm afraid you're flirting with me," she said.

"I'm afraid I am."

It was the stallion's fault. He stopped too suddenly. My hand slipped to her ankle. I kept it there.

I hadn't seen her move either, hadn't any idea how she had stopped the horse. He stood now like a casting in bronze.

She looked down very slowly at my hand on her ankle.

"Intentional?" she inquired.

"Very," I said.

"You have at least courage," she said. Her voice was distant, like a wood call. That kind of distance. I shook like a leaf.

She leaned down very very slowly until her head was almost as low as mine. The stallion didn't seem to move a muscle of his great body.

"I could do three things," she said. "Guess them."

"Easy. Ride on, use the whip on me, or just laugh."

"I was wrong," she said, in a suddenly taut voice. "Four things."

"Give me your lips," I said.

2.

The place appeared suddenly, down the slope from a wide, grassy circle, which was supposed to be what remained of a Roman camp. Down the slope was Lakeview, which, characteristically, had no view of the lake.

It lay in an utterness of neglect you don't see in England, in a jungle of tangled vines, a wilderness of long, weed-grown lawns. Even the sunken garden had become a pit of shame. Grass grew almost knee high on the Elizabethan bowling lawn at the side. The house itself was a lovely time-darkened red brick, in the traditional Elizabethan form, with outward-jutting, heavily leaded windows. Fat spiders slept behind them like bishops, and their webs mottled the glass, and they gazed out somnolently where once the hawk-faced dandies in slashed doublets had looked out at England, unappeased, in their furious days, by its cloistered charm.

Stables appeared, tottering in moss and neglect. A gnome, all hands and nose and riding breeches, came out of a shadowy stall and held the stallion.

She dropped to the bricks of the stable yard, walked away without a word.

"It's not neglect," she said, when we were out of the gnome's hearing. "It's simple murder. He knew I loved the place."

"Your husband?" I moved my lips softly, one inside the other, hating him.

"Let's go in the front way. You get the loveliest view of the main staircase. He excelled himself there. He gave that his personal attention."

There was a wide space in front, ringed with a drive. Ancient oaks closed it in. Its turf was worse than the rest because it had been scythed roughly and looked yellow. The oaks sent long shadows stealing insidiously across the ruined lawn, silent, dark, probing fingers of hate. Shadows, yet more than shadows, as the shadow on a sundial is more than a shadow.

A crone as aged and badly hung together as the stable gnome answered the remote, fretful jangling of the bell. The English of her sort seem never to go into a house. They must be admitted. The old woman muttered to herself in some obscure dialect, as though laying curses.

We stepped through the door, and the riding crop went up again.

"Now there," she said, in a voice than which nothing was ever harder, "you have his best work in the middle period, as painters say. Sir Henry Lakenham, Baronet, mind you, and please remember that a baronet is much more than a baron or viscount in our regard—Sir Henry Lakenham, one of our oldest baronets and one of our oldest staircases, meeting on somewhat unequal terms."

"You mean the ax was new," I said.

The main staircase, or what was left of it, was before us. It had been built for a royal descent, for a great lady with a retinue in velvet and stars, for an ingenuity of shadows on the vast paneled ceiling, for a victory or a triumph or a homecoming, and for, on occasion, just a staircase.

It was enormously broad and sweeping, it had the slow, indomitable curve of time. The balustrade alone must have been worth a fortune, but I merely guessed that. It had been hacked to jagged, dark splinters.

I turned away from it after quite a long time. There was a name now from which my stomach would always recoil.

"Wait a minute," I said. "You're still his—"

"Oh, that's part of the revenge."

The crone had gone mumbling away.

"What did you do to him?"

At first she said nothing. Then, very negligently: "I only wish I could do it again and again, forever, and that he might always hear of it down the dark places he will ultimately wander in."

"You don't mean that. Not all of it."

"No? Let's go this way. Our Romneys are famous—for their absence."

We went along what might have been a picture gallery. There were darker, plum-colored oblongs on the damask of the walls. Our footsteps echoed on a bare, dusty floor.

"Swine!" I said to the echoes and the emptiness. "Swine!"

"You don't really care," she said. "Do you?"

"No," I said. "Not as much as I pretend."

Beyond the gallery there was what might have been a gun room. From that a narrow, secret door led to a narrow, secret staircase, curved and intimate and gracious. We went up that. So we came at last to a room that was at least furnished.

She pulled her hard black hat off and fluffed her hair carelessly and threw her hat and gloves and whip on a bench. There was a huge canopied bed. Charles the Second had probably slept in it—not alone. There was a dressing table with wing mirrors and the usual chorus of glittering bottles. She went past all this, without a glance, to a table in the corner where she mixed Scotch and soda, tepid of course, and came back with two glasses in her hands.

Sinewy hands, the hands of a horsewoman. Not the lovely plastic things that were the hands of Millicent Crandall. These were hands that could be desperately tight, that could hurt. That could take a hunter over an impossible fence or a man over an aching abyss. Hands that almost shattered the fragile glasses she held. I saw their knuckles, as white as new ivory.

I was standing just inside the big old door and hadn't moved a muscle since I stepped into the room. She handed me a drink. It shook a little, and danced in the glass.

Her eyes—they were those far-off, unobtainable eyes. Those ancient eyes. They say nothing, they are utterly withdrawn. They are the last window that never opens in a house otherwise not secret.

Somewhere, I suppose, there was still the rather distant scent of sweet peas in an English garden, nectarines on a sunny wall, another fragrance and another head.

I reached back clumsily and turned the huge key, as big as a monkey wrench, in a lock the size of a cupboard door.

The lock creaked and we didn't laugh. We drank. Before I could put my glass down she was pressed against me so tightly that I stopped breathing.

Her skin was sweet and wild, like wildflowers on a sun baked slope, in spring, in the hard white sun of my own country. Our lips burned together, almost fused. Then hers opened and her tongue drove hard against my teeth and her body shook convulsively.

"Please," she said in a strangled voice, her mouth buried in mine. "Please, oh please—"

There could be only one ending.

3.

I don't remember what time it was when I got back to the Crandalls' cottage. I had to put a time on it afterward, for a reason, but I never really knew. The English summer afternoons last, like the English themselves, forever. I knew that Old Bessie was back because I could hear her humming monotone in the kitchen, like a fly caught in a pane of glass.

Perhaps even the almost infinite hour of tea had not been laid away.

I turned from the foot of the stairs and made myself go into the drawing room. That which I carried with me was neither all triumph nor all defeat, but it seemed to have no place there, where Millicent was.

She stood there, of course, as if waiting for me, her back to the futile lace curtains at the French doors. They were still, as she was. There was not, for the moment, enough life in the air to move them. She stood as if she had been waiting for silent, immobile hours. I felt somehow that the light had scarcely stirred along her arm or in the almost shadow of her throat.

She didn't say anything at once. Her not saying anything seemed very thunderous. Then her marble-smooth voice said, surprisingly, "You've loved me for three years now, haven't you, John?"

That was very swell, that was.

"Yes," I said. It was too late, far too late to be saying anything at all.

"I always knew it. You meant me to know it, didn't you, John?"

"I suppose so. Yes." The croak I heard seemed to be my voice.

Her pale blue eyes were placid as a pond under a full moon.

"I've always liked knowing it," she said.

I didn't move nearer to her. I just stood there, not exactly toeing holes in the carpet.

Quite suddenly, in that still, greenish late-afternoon light her frail body began to ripple from head to foot.

There was another silence. I did nothing to end it. At last she reached out to the frayed bell cord. The bell tinkled at the back of the house like a child crying.

"Well, we can always have tea," she said.

I got out of the room, as one does, without seeming to use the door.

I made the stairs without a fumble this time, the whole straight flight and the turn. But I was another man now. I was a smooth, quiet little man who had been put in his place and didn't matter at all, but wouldn't have anything to worry about either. All taken care of. Finished. A little man about two feet high who rolled his eyes when you shook him hard enough. Put him back in his box, dear, and let's go riding.

Then, just at the very top, where there was no step at all, I stumbled, and as if that made a draught, a door fell open, softly, like a leaf falling. Just half-open. Edward Crandall's bedroom door.

He was in there. The bed inside the door was very high and had at least two eiderdown mattresses on it, as they have in that part of the country. That was all I really looked at—the bed. He was sprawled all over it, on his face, as if eating it. Dead drunk. Passed out. A little early, even for him.

I stood there in the elf light that was neither afternoon nor dusk and looked in at him. The big black handsome brute, the conquering one. Filthy drunk, before it was even dark.

To hell with him. I reached over softly and shut the door again and almost tiptoed on to my own room, and washed up in the hand basin, with cold water. How cold it was, as cold as the morning after a battle.

I groped down the stairs again. In the meantime, tea had been served. She sat behind the low table, behind the large, polished urn, holding a sleeve away from it as she poured, so that her bare white arm seemed to shoot out of the sleeve.

"You must be tired," she said. "You must be terribly hungry," she said, in that flat, offhand, utterly dead voice that reminded me of the leave trains at Victoria during the war, the careless English women on the platform by the first-class carriages, saying those unimportant things, so easily, to the faces they would never see again. So careless, so smooth, so utterly dead inside.

It was like that. I took a cup of tea and a piece of scone.

"He's upstairs," I said. "Blotto. Of course you know that."

"Oh, yes." Her sleeve swirled a little, very delicately.

"Do I put him to bed?" I asked. "Or do I just let him decompose where he is?"

Her head jerked queerly. There was for the moment an expression she never meant me to see.

"John!" Quite smooth again now. "You've never talked like that about him before."

"Never talked much about him at all," I said. "Funny. He asked me down, too. And I came. Funny people—people are. It's been nice here too. I'm leaving."

"John!"

"The hell with it," I said. "I'm leaving. Thank him—when he's sober. Thank him a lot for asking me."

"John!" For the third time, just like that. "Aren't you being just a little strange?"

"It's the American gutturals creeping out," I said, "after a long hibernation."

"Have you hated him so much?"

"If you'll pardon an old friend," I said. "There are too many exclamation points in this conversation. Forget my bad manners. Of course I'll put him to bed—and then I'll take myself some English air."

But she was hardly listening to me now. She was leaning forward, and her eyes had an almost clairvoyant look, and she began to talk quickly, as if something had to be said and there wasn't much time and interruptions might come.

"There's a woman over at Lakeview," she said. "A Lady Lakenham. A terrible woman. A man-eater. He's been seeing her. This morning they had some sort of quarrel. He shouted all this at me, while we were alone in the house, contemptuously, over glasses of brandy he spilled all down his coat. She hit him in the face with a whip and rode him down on her horse."

Of course I wasn't hearing her either, not with my conscious ears. Instantly, as you'd snap your fingers, I had become a wooden man. It was as if all time were distilled into one instant and I had swallowed that, like a pill. It had made a wooden man of me. I could even feel a wooden grin pulling my face.

So even there he had to be first.

She stopped talking, it seemed, and she was looking at me across the tea urn. I saw her. I could see. One can, even in those moments. Her hair was ever so pale, her melancholy ever so distinct. She made the usual motions, slow, lovely curves of the arm and hand and wrist and cheek, which at the time had an almost unbearable seductiveness, but which in retrospect would have only the faded and uncertain grace of wisps of mist.

It seemed that I had handed her my cup and she was pouring me more tea.

"She lashed him with a hunting crop," she said. "Imagine! Edward! Then she rode him down, knocked him over with her big horse."

"On a big black stallion," I said. "She rode him down like a bundle of dirty rags."

Her breath caught in the stillness.

"Yes, she has her points," I said brutally. "And she loves the house. Lakeview. You ought to see what Lakenham did to the inside of it. He did his best lick on the main staircase—somebody else's heel of a husband."

Did her breath stay caught, or did someone laugh behind an arras, some court fool hiding from a wicked king?

"I knew her too," I said. "Intimately."

It seemed to dawn on her a little too slowly, as if a native had to be waked in a grass hut in Sumatra, and then run mile after mile through the jungle, and then a man had to ride a horse across a vast desert, and then a sailing ship had to battle storm after storm around the Horn, bringing the news home. It seemed to take all that time.

Her eyes got very large and very still and like gray glass. There was no color in them and no light.

"He must have thought he had the morning," I said. "I had an afternoon appointment. It just didn't—" I stopped. That wasn't funny, not in any company.

I stood up. "I'm sorry. So uselessly sorry. I'm just as easy to take as the next guy, for all my visions. I'm sorry. Sorry, and I know it's just a word."

She stood up too. She was coming around the table, very slowly. We were quite close together then, but no part of us touched.

Then she touched my sleeve, very lightly, as though a butterfly had lighted on it, and I was very still, not wanting to frighten the butterfly.

It floated away. It hovered in midair. It settled once more on my sleeve. Her voice said, as softly as the butterfly had moved. "We don't have to talk about it. We understand. We understand everything, you and I. We don't have to say a word."

"It could happen to anybody," I said. "The hell of it is when it does."

There was something else behind her eyes. They were not blank any more, but neither were they soft. Little doors were opening far back, at the ends of dark corridors. Doors that had been shut so long. So unutterably long. Steps came, along a stone corridor. They shuffled, without haste, without hope. A thread of smoke was caught in a draught and spiraled to nothing. All these things I seemed to see and know behind her eyes. Nonsense, of course.

"You're mine," she whispered, "all mine now."

She clutched my head and pulled it down. Her lips fumbling unskillfully on my mouth were as cold and remote as Arctic snow.

"Go upstairs and see if he is all right," she whispered secretly, "before you go."

"Sure." I spoke like a man who has been shot through the lungs.

So I went out of that room again, and up those stairs again.

Fumbling this time, fumbling with ancient caution. An old man whose bones were brittle. I got to my room and shut the door. I panted against it for a little while. Then I changed my clothes and put on the only lounge suit I had with me, tucked the rest of my stuff into a suitcase, closed the suitcase, and locked it very softly. Listening, moving very softly, a little boy who has been bad, bad, bad.

And in the silence I helped to make, steps came up the stairs and went into a room and came out of a room and went down the stairs again. Very slowly, all this, creeping like my thoughts.

Sounds came back. The cracked, incessant humming of the old woman in the kitchen, the buzzing of a late bee under my window, the creaking of an old countryman's cart far down the road. I picked up my suitcase and went out of my room. I shut its door softly, softly.

And at the top of the stairs *his* door had to be wide open again. Wide open, as if somebody had come up deliberately and opened it and left it open.

I put the suitcase down and leaned against the wall and stared in. He didn't seem to have moved much. Pretty complete case. He looked as if he had taken a running dive onto the high bed and grabbed two big handfuls of the counterpane and so passed into the large alcoholic beyond.

Then in the gray stillness I was aware of a lack of sound. The stertorous breathing, half snore, half mutter of the unconscious drunk. I listened—oh, very carefully. It was missing—his breathing. He didn't make any sound at all, sprawled on his face on that high bed.

Yet it wasn't even that that brought me into the room like a panther, crouching, noiseless, holding my own breath. It was something I had already looked at and not observed. His left ring finger. Funny, that was. It was half an inch longer than the middle finger next to it, as his hand hung limp against the spread. It should have been half an inch shorter.

It was half an inch longer. The extra length happened to be a congealed icicle of blood.

It had come all the way from his throat, soundless, implacable, and made that funny icicle there.

He had been dead, of course, for hours.

4.

I shut the door of the drawing room very politely, very care-fully, like an old family priest departing into his funk hole, in the days of one of the anti-Catholic persecutions.

Then I stole over and shut the French doors. I suppose a little last fragrance of the roses and the nectarines crept in at me, mockingly, as I did this.

She was leaning back in a low chair, smoking a cigarette not skillfully, her pale gold head against a cushion. Her eyes—I didn't know what was in her eyes. I had had enough of what was in eyes, anyhow.

"Where's the gun? It should be in his hand."

I made it sharp but not loud, not a carrying voice. But there was no gentle English grayness in me now.

She smiled very faintly and pointed to one of those spindly articles of furniture on insecure logs which sometimes have drawers but are really to hold an array of little glazed cups and mugs emblazoned in gilt: "A Present from Bognor Regis," or wherever it was, and a coat of arms.

This particular sideboy, or whatever it was, had a stiff curved drawer, which I pulled out, rattling the glazed mugs a little.

It was in there, on a sheet of pink shelf paper, against a fringed doily. A Webley revolver. Innocent as a fish knife.

I put my nose down and sniffed at it. There seemed to be that harsh smell of cordite. I didn't touch the gun—yet.

"So you knew," I said. "You knew all the time I was making a prissy fool of myself. You knew while we had tea. You knew he was lying up there on that bed. Dripping blood slowly, slowly, slowly—the dead *do* bleed, but so slowly—from a wound in his throat, down under his shirt, down his arm, down his hand, down his finger. You knew all the time."

"That beast," she said in an utterly calm voice. "That offal. Have you any idea what he has subjected me to?"

"All right," I said. "I get that too. I'm not squeamish either, about his sort. But things have to be done. The gun shouldn't have been touched at all. Where it was it probably looked all right. Now you've handled it. Fingerprints, you know. You know about fingerprints?"

I wasn't talking to a child or being sarcastic either. I was just getting an idea over, in case it hadn't got over. She had somehow discarded the cigarette without my observing a movement. She could do those things. She sat now very still, her hands on the arms of her chair, slim, separate, as delicate as dawn.

"You were here alone," I said. "It was while Old Bessie had gone out. Nobody heard the shot, or would have thought of it as anything but a hunting gun."

She laughed then. It was a low, ecstatic laugh, the laugh of a woman nestling back among pillows, in a great canopied bed.

As she laughed, the lines of her throat sharpened a little. And they never softened again, that I saw.

"Why," she asked, "are you worrying about all that?"

"You should have told me before. What are you laughing at? Do you think this English law of yours is funny? . . . And you went up and opened that door—you. So I wouldn't leave without knowing. Why?"

"I loved you," she said. "After a fashion. I'm a cold woman, John. Did you know I was a cold woman?"

"I suspected it, but it didn't happen to be any of my business. You're not answering my question."

"Your business, as it were, lay elsewhere."

"That's a thousand years ago. Ten thousand. That lies with the Pharaohs. Crumbling in an ancient shroud. This is for now." I pointed upward, a hard stiff finger.

"It's beautiful," she sighed. "Let's not make a cheap sensation of it. It's a beautiful tragedy." She touched her slim, delicate neck caressingly.

"They'll hang me, John. They do—in England."

I stared at her with what eyes I had and what was in them.

"Deliberately," she said coolly. "With due formality. And some faint, summary regrets. And the governor of the prison will have a perfect crease in his trousers, put there as deliberately, as carefully, as coldly as—as I shot him."

I kept on breathing enough to stay alive. "On purpose?" It was a useless question. I already knew.

"Of course. I've been intending to for months. Today seemed somehow a little more brutal than usual. This woman over at Lakeview didn't improve his self-esteem. She made him cheap. He was always nasty. So I did what I did."

"But you could stand his being just nasty," I said.

She nodded that head. I heard a strange, clanking noise like nothing else on earth. Something swayed, hooded. Very gently it swayed, in a cold light, from a long, hidden exquisite neck.

"No," I said, without breath. "Never. This is easy. Will you play it my way?"

She stood up all in one smooth motion and came to me. I took her in my arms. I kissed her. I touched her hair.

"My knight," she whispered. "My plumed knight. My glistening one."

"How?" I asked, pointing into the drawer at the gun. "They'll test his hand for powder nitrates. That is, leakage of gas when the gun is fired. It's something that stays in the skin for a while and makes a chemical reaction. That has to be arranged."

She stroked my hair. "They will, my love. They will find what you mean. I put the gun in his own hand, and held it there, and soothed him. My finger was over his finger. He was so drunk he didn't even know what he was doing."

She went on stroking my hair.

"My plumed, glistening knight," she said.

I wasn't holding her now; she was holding me. I squeezed my brains slowly, slowly. Into a clot.

"It may not make a very good test," I said. "And they might test your hand as well. So we must do two things. Are you listening to me?"

"My plumed knight!" Her eyes shone.

"You must wash your right hand with good, harsh laundry soap and hot water, for a long time. It may hurt, but keep it up as long as you dare without taking the skin off. That would show. I mean that. It's important. The other thing is—I'm leaving with the gun. That should throw them off. I don't think that nitrate test is any good after about forty-eight hours. Understand?"

She said the same things, in the same way, and her eyes shone with the same light. Her hand on my head was the same soft, lingering hand.

I didn't hate her. I didn't love her. It was just something I had to do. I got the Webley and the pink paper under it, because that was slightly oil-stained. I looked closely at the wood of the drawer. That seemed clean. I put the gun and the paper away in my pockets.

"You don't sleep in the room with him," I pounded on. "He's drunk—sleeping it off. Nothing new, nothing to get excited or worried about. You heard a shot, of course, at somewhere around the right time, but not too close and not too evasive either. You thought it was a gun in the woods."

She held my arm. I had to smooth hers. Her eyes demanded it.

"You're pretty disgusted with him," I said. "It's happened often enough, so that you got an overload today. So he's to be left alone till morning. Then Old Bessie—"

"Oh, not Old Bessie," she said beautifully. "Not poor Old Bessie."

It may have been a nice touch. It slid past me. I started to go.

"The main things—washing your hand, but not enough to inflame it—and me off with the gun. All set?"

She clutched me again, with that fierce, unskillful clutch.

"And afterwards—?"

"And afterwards—" I breathed dreamily against her icy lips.

I pried myself loose from her and left that house.

5.

For almost three weeks I stayed clear of them, or they let me. I was pretty good, for an amateur, in a small tight country like England.

I ditched my runabout late at night, in the loneliest copse I could drive to without lights. It seemed a thousand wind-swept solitary miles from anywhere. It wasn't, of course. I dragged my suitcase across infinite English landscapes, through the dark, through fields of drowsy cattle, past the fringes of silent villages where not a single lamp warmed the night.

Not too early I reached a railway station and rode it to London. I knew where to go, a small lodging house in Bloomsbury, north of Russell Square, a place where no one was what he should be or wanted to be, and no one cared, least of all the slattern who called herself the landlady.

Breakfast, a cold, greasy mess on a tray outside your door. Lunch, ale and bread and cheddar, if you wanted it. Dinner, if you were in the dining class, you went out and foraged for. If you came home late at night, the white-faced specters of Russell Square haunted you, creeping along where the iron railings had been, as though the mere memory of them brought some shelter from the policeman's lantern. They haunted you all night with the ache of their "Listen, dearies," with the remembrance of their pinched lips, gnawed thin from within, their large hollow eyes in which a world was already dead.

There was a man at the digs who played Bach, a little too much and a little too loud; but he did it for his own soul.

There was a lonely old man with a poised, delicate face and a filthy mind. There were two young wooden butterflies who thought of themselves as actors.

I got sick of all that soon enough. I bought a knapsack and went on a walking tour down to Devonshire. I was in the papers, of course, but not prominently. No sensation, no blurred reproduction of my passport photograph, which made me look like an Armenian rug merchant with the toothache. Just a discreet paragraph about my being missing, age, height, weight, color of eyes, American, believed to have information which might aid the authorities. There was some brief biographical stuff about Edward Crandall, not more than three lines. He was not important to them. Merely a well-to-do man who happened to be dead. Calling me an American clinched it. My accent, when I tried it, was almost good enough for Bloomsbury. It would be more than good enough for the rural districts.

They caught up with me at Chagford, near the edge of Dartmoor. I was having tea, of course, the parlor boarder at a small farmhouse, a writer down from London for a bit of a rest. Nice manners, but no talker. Fond of cats.

They had two fat ones, a black and a white, who liked Devonshire cream as much as I did. The cats and I had our tea together. It was a dismal afternoon, as gray as a prison yard. A hangman's day. Mists would be hanging in low clumps on the hard yellow gorse of the moor.

There were two of them, a Constable Tressider, local man, though with a Cornish name, and the Scotland Yard man. This one was the enemy. The local man merely sat in the corner and smelled of his uniform.

The other was fiftyish, beautifully built, as they are over there when they are, red-faced, a warrant officer of the Guards without the ruthless, deadly detached voice. He was soft and quiet and friendly. He put his hat on the far end of the long dinner table and picked up the black cat.

"Glad to find you in, sir. Inspector Knight from the Yard. You've given us a very nice run for our money."

"Have tea," I said. I went over to pull the bell and leaned against the wall. "Have tea—with a murderer."

He laughed. Constable Tressider did not laugh. His face expressed nothing but the bitter wind on the moor.

"Gladly—but we won't talk of that other now, if you please. But just to ease your mind—nobody's in any real trouble over the affair."

I must have turned pretty white. He jumped for a bottle of Dewar's on the mantle and shook some of it into a glass faster than I would have thought such a big man could have moved. He had it against my mouth. I gulped.

A hand felt me over, a hand as neat and questing as a hummingbird's bill, as sharp, as thorough.

I grinned at him. "You'll have it," I said. "I just don't wear it to tea."

The constable had his tea in the corner, and the Scotland Yard man at the table, with the black cat in his lap. Rank, after all, is rank.

I went back to London with him that same evening.

And there was nothing to it—absolutely nothing.

They had been foxed and they knew it, and as the English always do, they lost as if they were winning. Outwardly, it was, why had I taken the gun? Because she had foolishly handled it, and that frightened me. Oh yes, I see. But it would really have been much better—you see, the Crown—and the inquest being adjourned at the request of the police makes a hint of something wrong, don't you think? I thought so, contritely.

That was outwardly. Inwardly, I saw it behind the cold gray stone walls of their eyes. The idea had come to them just too late and it was my fault. Just too late had arrived in their bleak, keen minds the possibility of his being just drunk enough and just silly enough to let somebody put a gun in his hand and point it (where he couldn't see it) and say "Bang!" and make him pull the trigger, with a finger over his lax finger, and then let him fall back—not laughing.

I saw Millicent Crandall at the adjourned inquest, a woman in black I had met somewhere, long ago. We did not speak to each other. I never saw her again. She must have looked ravishing in black chiffon nightgowns. She could wear one now, any day or any year.

I saw Lady Lakenham once, in Piccadilly, by the Green Park, strolling with a man and a dog. She sent them on and stopped. I think the dog was some sort of bob-tailed sheep-dog type, but much smaller. We shook hands. She looked marvelous.

We stood in the middle of the sidewalk, and the English moved around us meticulously, as the English do.

Her eyes were black marble, opaque, calm, at peace.

"You were swell to go to bat for me," I said.

"Why, darling, I had the grandest time with the Assistant Commissioner at Scotland Yard. The whole place simply swam with Scotch and soda."

"Without you," I said, "they might have tried to pin it on me."

"Tonight," she said, very quickly, very busily, "I'm terribly afraid I'm all booked up. But tomorrow—I'm staying at Claridge's. You'll call?"

"Tomorrow," I said. "Oh, definitely." (I was leaving England tomorrow.) "So you rode him down on Romeo. I'm being impertinent. Why?"

This on Piccadilly, by the Green Park, while the careful pedestrians eddied.

"Did I? Why, how utterly abominable of me. Don't you know why?" A thrush, as calm as the Green Park itself.

"Of course," I said. "Men of his type make that mistake. They think they own every woman who smiles at them." The wild perfume of her skin came to me a little, as if a desert wind brought it a thousand miles to me.

"Tomorrow," she said. "About four. You needn't even telephone, really."

"Tomorrow," I lied.

I stared at her until she was quite out of sight. Motionless, utterly motionless. They moved around me politely, those English, as though I were a monument, or a Chinese sage, or a life-sized doll in Dresden china.

Quite motionless. A chill wind blew leaves and bits of paper across the now lusterless grass of Green Park, across the trim walks, almost over the high curbing into Piccadilly itself.

I stood there for what seemed a long, long time, looking after nothing. There was nothing to look after.

◈